Acclaim for

ZONEfulness®

THE ULTIMATE GUIDE FOR STUDENT-ATHLETES

"I have been playing basketball my entire life, but it wasn't until college, where the stakes were higher, that I struggled immensely with performance anxiety. I would get onto the court and all of a sudden, my legs felt heavy and I had trouble breathing.

After implementing the strategies in ZONEfulness®, my life changed. I owe a large part of my success at Penn as a back-to-back Ivy League champion to Joe Dowling. I am beyond grateful! I recommend that if any athlete wants to take his or her game to the next level that they read his book and really believe in the power of his strategies. I promise it will be worth it!"

– Kasey Chambers, graduate assistant coach,
The George Washington University women's basketball team;
2016 and 2017 Ivy League champion and team captain of the
University of Pennsylvania women's basketball team

"The thing that I loved about the ZONEfulness® book is its accessibility. Joe masterfully takes complex concepts and techniques and presents them in ways that are easily understandable and immediately relatable. It stands out for me because it doesn't just tell you what, it shows you how. This makes the book a valuable tool for athletes, coaches, and sport psychology practitioners."

– Jaison Freeman, Ph.D, Doctor of Sport Psychology

"Coach Dowling's book is a must read for any athlete. Achieving peak performance is a critical component necessary to have success. Some key points within the book that resonated with me were: finding your zone; every play is the next play; the importance of visualizing your future memories of success; and always keeping a positive focus on what you've set out to achieve.

Coach Dowling's work with our team at Penn no doubt played a key role in us reaching our goal as Ivy League champions and playing in the NCAA Tournament. His work with us fostered a culture of accountability and togetherness. This book will provide insight and offers various tips and tricks on how to mentally outwork your competition and gain an edge."

> --Matt McDonald, Brooklyn Nets, basketball operations assistant; 2017 and 2018 Ivy League team captain of The University of Pennsylvania men's basketball team

---

"I'm so glad Joe turned ZONEfulness® into a book. The intense work we did together, I'm convinced, was the main reason I was able to advance through the minor leagues and finally play major league ball. For me, the Zone recordings were crucial! They helped me really master locking in to one pitch at a time. I require my high school team to read ZONEfulness® so they can learn to support themselves and be better teammates."

> – Mike Costanzo, head coach, Archbishop Carrol baseball team; 65th overall selection (second round) of 2005 Major League Baseball draft; made Major League debut with the Cincinnati Reds on May 13th, 2012

"Before reading ZONEfulness®, I never consistently practiced the mental part of my game. As a former chronic "what-ifer," I often found that my times of self-doubt significantly held me back from reaching my full potential in my sport. Through active practice, these concepts Joe introduced me to have helped me improve immensely as a Division I athlete, a professional, and an all-around person. I highly recommend this book to those looking to transform their mental game. My only regret is not reading it sooner."

> – Jurie Joyner, 2018 MVP of The University of Pennsylvania softball team

"Joe has been working with our entire team as well as training individual players since 2016. I have seen a significant shift in those who are 'all in' and really use his concepts. His book is a great read for players and coaches to understand how self-talk can hinder or propel them to success. Joe gives them the tools to be able to play in the now and focus fully on what they CAN do to meet their potential. "

> – Karin Corbett, Head Coach, The University of Pennsylvania women's lacrosse; 11 time Ivy League champion (2007-2018); 2 time NCAA final four participant (2007, 2009).

"My wife Maureen and I can't thank Joe enough for the incredible work and major impact his ZONEfulness® approach has had on our son, Owen. For the first time in his high school career, he was relaxed under pressure and able to perform at the highest level. More importantly, he learned to use the ZONEfulness® techniques to experience his most positive self and consistently envision successful outcomes both on the field and in all areas of his life. We highly recommend ZONEfulness® to all student-athletes and their parents!"

> – Mark McAdoo, former Division I baseball player and proud parent

---

"Joe's teachings have allowed me to reach my highest level of peak performance by enabling me to unleash my inner zone. The ZONEfulness® model and book have transformed my mindset in my golf game, as well as in my life. I would not be the athlete, and more importantly, the person, I am today without Joe and all of the guidance he has given me."

> – Carter Thompsen, three year starter for The University of Pennsylvania golf team.

"I first met Joe Dowling in 2016 after a rough freshman baseball season for The University of Pennsylvania. I hit a mere .230 and had failed for the first time in my life at baseball. I was left with doubt about my ability to play D-I ball and unsure of how to deal with failure. I met with Joe that summer and was introduced to his ZONEfulness® model. The following year I saw the benefits of our work; I improved significantly in every statistical offensive category and hit .323.

Joe helped me find confidence, but more importantly, I also found the consistency that has helped breed continued success throughout my college career. Without Joe and ZONEfulness® I don't think I would have been able to reach my potential. ZONEfulness® was the last and most significant piece to figuring out how good I could be."

– Sean Phelan, 2018 second team all-Ivy selection

"ZONEfulness®: The Ultimate Guide for Student-Athletes is a must read for athletes, student-athletes, coaches and athletic directors at every level. Sport Psychologist Joe Dowling does a phenomenal job teaching readers how to achieve peak mental performance, which in turn leads to peak physical performance by providing real-life examples and stories of such outcomes.

As a former Division I volleyball coach and current strength and conditioning coach for athletes of all ages and abilities, I utilize the strategies that Joe puts forth in his book. My student-athletes have used Joe's techniques to overcome personal issues such as serving errors or hitting slumps—and for team items like playing every point as if it were the first, and focusing on playing with confidence and envisioning success. ZONEfulness® techniques are also an incredible resource I utilize every day with the athletes I train and coach."

– Heather Hoehn, former head volleyball coach
at Villanova University and The University of Minnesota

"Joe Dowling's book, ZONEfulness® : The Ultimate Guide for Student-Athletes, mirrors what Joe does so well for my program. Namely, the book captures his ability to effectively teach peak performance techniques to student-athletes. More importantly, the stories throughout the book demonstrate how student-athletes not only buy-in to mental strength training but how they maximize their play by winning the mind game. Joe works with my team as a unit as well as individually throughout the season. His contribution is critical to our continued success as a program."

> – Mike McLaughlin, 2 time Ivy League Coach of the Year for The University of Pennsylvania women's basketball team; 500+ career wins

---

"Joe is my mental strength and peak performance coach here at Penn. He is an incredible resource who works with each player individually throughout the year and meets with the team 2-3 times a month for the entire season. I love the book not only because it shows student-athletes what to actually DO in order to consistently play at their highest level but because the same techniques can be applied to success in the classroom and in life. Joe taught ZONEfulness® to my teams at Boston College and Cornell before the book was written. Now that it's out there I know it will be of tremendous value to student-athletes and coaches on the high school and college levels."

> – Steve Donahue, men's basketball head coach, The University of Pennsylvania; 2018 Ivy League champions and Coach of the Year

ZONEfulness®
THE ULTIMATE GUIDE FOR STUDENT-ATHLETES

4 Techniques to Access and Master Your Zone

Copyright © 2017 by Joseph Dowling

All rights reserved. No part of this publication may be reproduced or transmitted in any form or by any means, electronic or mechanical, including photocopy, recording or any information storage and retrieval system without permission in writing from the publisher.

ISBN-13: 978-0-692-93061-8

First published in 2017
www.ZONEfulness.com

Cover photo:
TT Naslonski, 2022 Rutgers University
and
Matt Howard, 2017 University of Pennsylvania
Credit: Don E. Felice
Printed in the United States of America

To Lisa:

My foundation of endless inspiration. My ultimate guide. My love.

TABLE OF CONTENTS

INTRODUCTION... 13

PART 1:
ZONEfulness®: The Zone Lives Inside of You 17

    Chapter One: A Spontaneous Zone.. 19

    Chapter Two: A Zone Revelation 21

    Chapter Three: A Zone Exercise 23

    Chapter Four: "Where Did My Zone Go?" 25

Part II: ZONEfulness®:
The Big Three of Peak Performance and a Final Fourth Technique 43

    Chapter Five: Magnify the Good 45
    Technique #1:
    Personal History of Success

    Chapter Six: Love and Peace with Yourself----OR ELSE! 63
    Technique #2:
    Extreme Self-Support (Internal Strength)
    Support from Family, Friends, Coaches,
    and Teammates (External Strength)

    Chapter Seven: How to Dismantle an Atomic What-if........................... 91
    Technique #3:
    Future Memories of Success

    Chapter Eight: After Stepping into Yourself, Step-Out......................... 133
    The Final Fourth Technique:
    Gratitude and Giving Back

ZONEfulness®

INTRODUCTION

ZONEfulness®

I had an "Ah-ha" moment in March, 2014. I'm sure you've had the experience of an idea just crystalizing out of nowhere. The "Ah-ha" is often so perfect that you find yourself wondering what took so long for you to discover it.

I was struggling to define my unique, experiential approach to being in the zone with student-athletes. My style includes elements of meditation, visualization, and even some hypnotherapy. Inherent in this model is an emphasis on the strength and future potential of each client I treat. Essentially, I practice peak performance positive psychology.

But I knew I was doing more. I facilitate a sensory experience for student-athletes. In certain sessions, I guide them to recreate the zone they experience when competing at their highest level. These zone exercises are the catalyst that propel each individual to access and maintain their peak performance zone while competing in their sport.

Zone exercises also enable student-athletes to more easily implement the principles of positive psychology that enhance confidence and generate Extreme Self-Support. The zone exercises were initially characterized by an eyes closed, meditative state of relaxation. Subsequently, I began facilitating eyes open, active, alert zone experiences.

Incorporating eyes closed, relaxed zones with eyes open, alert zones enables clients to naturally translate their experience from my office to real-time play in their sport. This desired yet mysterious zone, manifested in competition, is now understood to be an accessible, powerful tool.

The student-athlete can, via specialized zone exercises and the principles of positive, strength-based psychology, rapidly step into the flow and confidence that characterizes their peak performance zone.

So what about this "Ah-ha" experience? I was reading an article on PhillySports.com about the Penn State University men's basketball team using mindfulness meditation as their primary tool for mental focus training.

Tim Frazier, Penn State's all-time leader in assists, describes his experience: "The game moves so fast, it's hard to focus on the here and now. Meditation slows me down [mentally], keeps me more relaxed and focused."

Michael Baime, an internist and director of the Penn Program for Mindfulness states, "Elite athletic performance is mostly a mental game. Mindfulness practice really isn't that different from athletic training. If you want to get neuroscientific about it, mindfulness practice changes the structure of the brain through which awareness operates. Just as running increases the strength of the quadriceps muscles, mindfulness practice strengthens the executive control function of the brain."

Mindfulness meditation is about being in the moment. Specifically, it focuses on the experience of breathing and stillness. If a thought interferes with the experience, the meditator is encouraged to be curious and accepting while refocusing on each comfortable breath.

Zone exercises enhance perception and sensation. Revivification of the sights, sounds, and feelings of past successes and the magnification of future achievements are routinely experienced in this experiential process.

Mindfulness meditation is a critical element of the zone exercises. It provides a calming, peaceful space for student-athletes to experience prior to exploring, for example, their Personal History of Success zone; their Future Memories of Success zone; or their Extreme Self-Support zone. The mindfulness meditative state is a foundational element to the peak performance zone exercises I facilitate for clients.

And then it hit me: ZONEfulness®!

ZONEfulness® is the integration of mindfulness meditation, peak performance zone exercises, and positive psychology. This book is a profoundly simple guide designed for student-athletes to generate and maintain peak performance by accessing the zone that lives inside of them.

Finally, please enjoy the experience this book has to offer. You will have the opportunity to immediately exercise your zone and incorporate powerfully calm ZONEfulness® techniques into your athletic performance, and your life . . .

ZONEfulness®

4 Techniques to Access and Master Your Zone

PART ONE

ZONEfulness®

CHAPTER ONE
A SPONTANEOUS ZONE

LaSalle College High School, Philadelphia, PA
Freshman Basketball Game
LaSalle versus Cardinal Dougherty

Play-by-play announcer: "Rebound goes to LaSalle's Rodden, outlet pass to Greenberg, he dribbles over midcourt, passes to Dowling on the left wing; he drives the lane to the basket. It's good, and he's fouled on the play. Let's see if he can complete the 3-point play at the free throw line."

The preceding account was how I imagined the play-by-play announcer would have called the first play of my first game as a high school basketball player. The play actually happened but there was no announcer in the LaSalle gymnasium.

As a matter of fact, there were approximately 50 people watching the game, including both teams. Nevertheless, this was for me the NBA Championship, the Super Bowl, and the Olympic Gold Medal all rolled into one.

Playing basketball at LaSalle College High School was a dream come true. This initial game a monumental, life changing event. I was 13-years-old, in 9th grade, and awed and overwhelmed at this moment in time. And now I stood at the free throw line. And I froze.

I received the ball from the official and began my regular routine: five dribbles; one deep breath; knees bent; look at the front of the rim; shoot. But, this time . . . I couldn't shoot. I was immobilized—stuck in this moment.

A palpable wave of fear flowed through me for a few seconds. Then I locked in on the front of the rim, a tunnel vision developed, more time elapsed. I now felt a rush of calm, a confidence.

Play-by-play announcer: Dowling sure is taking his time. He shoots, it's good. He completes the 3-point play.

I later learned that almost ten seconds had elapsed from the time I had received the ball to the moment I released the shot, an insufferable amount of time to complete a free throw.

So what happened? I lapsed into a spontaneous zone; a state of extreme focus and concentration that dissolved my fear and anxiety. This miraculous occurrence was for my 13-year-old self the catalyst to continue shooting free throws using my original routine, with one exception: From this point forward I would now take up to ten seconds to stare at the front of the rim and experience the confidently calm expectation of success that my newfound free throw zone provided.

Epilogue: I continued to shoot free throws in this manner through the next two seasons, even though it greatly annoyed opposing teams and fans. It even bothered my teammates at times. It wasn't until my junior year that I started to worry about how I was perceived by fans, teammates . . . well, everyone.

Desiring to blend in, I abandoned my lengthy free throw style for the first five games of the season. Rapidly, my shooting percentage plummeted from 87% to 68%. My coach not-so-gently requested (demanded) I return to "the longer foul shot routine." When I honored his request I reconnected with my familiar focus and success at the free throw line. Once again, I could enjoy the peaceful flow that foul shooting provided me. If only I could transport this confidence, focus, and calm into all areas of my life.

CHAPTER TWO
A ZONE REVELATION

**Villanova University Master's in Counseling Program, Villanova, PA
Creativity in Counseling Class, 1990**

Dr. Nicholas Rosa: "Dr. Milton H. Erickson taught that everyone has a conscious mind and a subconscious mind. The conscious mind is very good at analyzing and organizing. However, it frequently creates symptoms of anxiety, notably obsessive thinking and worrying. The subconscious mind is an infinite storehouse of learnings, potentials and possibilities. The subconscious mind is where you go when you are in a zone, or as Dr. Erickson stated, 'a naturalistic trance.' "

The zone is an absorbed, focused state of attention and control. It is a natural state of mind-body connection that bypasses the limitations of the conscious, thinking mind and magnifies the abilities of the subconscious mind.

The zone lives in the subconscious mind and is something that people naturally experience all the time, typically without even knowing it. Examples include: Athletic activities (jump shooting, pitching, running, receiving, passing, ice skating, javelin throwing, etc.); painting or writing; daydreaming; reading; watching a movie.

The list of absorbing activities that people experience is seemingly endless and is characterized by not only a focused state of control, but feelings of relaxation, confidence, and timelessness.

ZONEfulness®

As the semester progressed I was becoming more familiar with accessing the inner zone that lives in my subconscious. I was learning how to help people tap in to their zone, to dip down beneath the chatter and clatter of their over-thinking mind.

LaSalle versus Cardinal Dougherty, 1978: Play-by-play announcer: "Dowling sure is taking his time. He shoots, it's good!"

I know now what I didn't know then: That my subconscious mind took over. It enabled me to zone in, to bypass the frozen fear, to create extraordinary focus and confidence, and to make the shot. Now I know how to take people to that natural state of flow.

As a specialist in peak performance and positive psychology I have been training student-athletes for 20 years on how to access and maintain their peak performance zone. I call my approach ZONEfulness®. This book teaches ZONEfulness® techniques that will enable student-athletes to generate and accelerate maximum performance. Symptoms of anxiety, challenges, and obstacles will be transformed into positive triggers; powerful reminders to automatically reconnect with the zone that lives on the inside.

LaSalle versus Cardinal Dougherty, 1978: Revised voice of play-by-play announcer: "Dowling is zoning in. He shoots, it's good! Was there ever a doubt?"

CHAPTER THREE
A ZONE EXERCISE

**My Home Office, the Manayunk Section of Philadelphia, PA
4th Sport Psychology Session with Owen, a 17-Year-Old
High School Junior, Preparing for the Upcoming Baseball Season,
March, 2013**

Owen: "When can we do the zone? I'm getting great at going really fast into it. I've been listening to the recordings we've made and doing the one minute power zone like, five times a day."

Owen loves baseball. He was extremely concerned that he wasn't improving at the pace he had always imagined. Approaching the start of his junior year high school baseball season he was considered just a slightly above-average player. During his sophomore year his batting average was .275, with 2 home runs, 10 doubles, and 1 triple. He was considered just an average first baseman.

Owen told me in our first session in January, 2013, that he was "really worried" that he wouldn't be a starter on the team that season. I soon noticed that he was starting to speak rapidly, a bit louder, and his breathing was becoming strained. He was questioning everything: "What-If I get cut? What-If I don't start? I really sucked last year, why couldn't I hit the fastball? I know this year will be worse! Why am I in this position? It's my junior year!"

During the first five minutes of his first session Owen nailed the three most common zone blockers, or symptoms, (self-criticism, what-ifing, why-ning) that prevent athletes from getting into their zone. I learned that his pattern of negative thinking had started in little league and was only becoming worse.

As I listened to Owen voice his frustration I felt it was the right time to change the energy in the room. I told him I had a really simple and interesting exercise, a zone exercise, that would enable him to reconnect with all the success and fun he's had playing baseball over the years. I then guided him to close his eyes and take five very slow, very deep breaths. I invited him to be curious as he focused his attention and stared at the light on the inside of his eyes.

Over the next 15 minutes I led him into his zone, what I now call a state of ZONEfulness®, and suggested that he vividly remember the sights, sounds, sensations, and feelings of his achievements on the diamond; that he hear the sound of supportive voices, like coaches, teammates, family, and friends, as well as his own voice supporting teammates; and finally, that he launch himself forward in time to the upcoming season and experience the ping of the bat, the home runs, the doubles, the pop of the ball into his first baseman's mitt, and the feelings of confidence and fun that await him.

Owen opened his eyes with a peaceful, calm expression of comfort. He felt that the experience had been "3 or 4 minutes" in duration. I assured him that he had lost track of time on countless occasions in the past, specifically whenever he was zoned in, and not just on the baseball field. He was in a zone when reading, listening to music, working out, watching a movie, or any time he was deeply focused.

He nodded to this understanding and began to ask a question. His speech was clear and steady, his breathing balanced, and his expression seemed comfortably curious. "So, Mr. Dowling, where did my zone go last year, and how can I find it this season?"

4th Sport Psychology Session with Owen, March, 2013

Owen: "When can we do the zone? I'm getting great at going really fast into it. I've been listening to the recordings we've made and doing the one minute power zone like, five times a day.

Can you believe in my first session that I asked you where my zone went? I can't wait for the season to start."

CHAPTER FOUR
"WHERE DID MY ZONE GO?"

"When I step onto the court, I don't have to think about anything. If I have a problem off the court, I find that after I play, my mind is clearer and I can come up with a better solution. It's like therapy. It relaxes me and allows me to solve problems."
— Michael Jordan, Legendary Hall of Fame Basketball Player

I have always loved playing and watching sports. Basketball is my first passion, an all-consuming focus that began at the age of six. Hoops was certainly my favorite, however, I played baseball, football, tennis, soccer, ice hockey, golf—really anything that was available to me and my friends.

Throughout elementary school I actually believed that my career path had me ticketed to be an NBA point guard. This unwavering belief of future professional stardom was shattered shortly after starting high school.

Nevertheless, as I came crashing back to reality, I realized that I could at least play varsity basketball and baseball. In retrospect, my memories are extraordinary. Most notably, the fun of practicing and playing games, the camaraderie and relationships (many of which continue to this day), and the achievement of being a starting player on some excellent teams. I was even fortunate enough to continue my career playing for a small Division III college basketball team.

What about the other memories? I look back now and understand that if there had been a sport known as self-criticizing or what-ifing, I would have unquestionably been an all-American. I had an inner, negative voice that was always chattering and complaining about everything that I was doing wrong and anything that could go wrong.

Actually, I was a happy, well-adjusted kid, yet this inner dialogue was exhausting. But the negativity would dissolve whenever I played well. I would waver between being zoned in and beating myself up. A successful jump shot or a steal and a breakaway layup would infuse confidence. A missed shot or a turnover would trigger self-criticism and dissolve my zone. *So where did my zone go?*

The College Scout—A Shattered Zone

Now, I must emphasize that playing on the LaSalle basketball team brought me great joy. I truly value that experience and I fully understand how it helped me to grow and mature as a young man while delivering lasting memories. I wish I knew then what I know now—specifically, how to bypass and dissolve the bouts of self-criticism and negativity that swept away my zone.

In the days long before e-mail and text messaging, I received a letter on Christmas Eve. I was the starting LaSalle High School point guard and playing very well. The team had played approximately ten games into my senior year. We were highly touted, primarily because of our all-American, do-everything player, Chip Greenberg. All of the attention Chip was getting meant that my teammates and I had the chance to be noticed and evaluated by college scouts.

So when I received that letter from Coach Tom Finnegan, the head basketball coach at Washington College in Chestertown, Maryland, I was blown away; ecstatic. He had seen me play at a holiday tournament and wanted to take a trip up to Philadelphia to see me play again. What an opportunity!

I responded to coach Finnegan and confirmed that his attending the January game against Bishop McDevitt would be great and that I was looking forward to meeting him.

4 Techniques to Access and Master Your Zone

> *"Overthinking is holding your breath and clenching all your muscles." — Stephen Gilligan, Zone Expert*

I was pumped! We won the next three games and I played very well. I was running the offense, getting the ball to the hot hand, and scoring a bit more than my average. I was all over the court. My confidence was high. And then I started thinking.

I knew the next game wasn't just another game. The next game was Bishop McDevitt. Coach Finnegan would be there, critiquing my performance, determining my future.

I vividly remember not sleeping well the night before the game. I felt disconnected and uneasy in class that day. Then the what-ifs began to escalate and reverberate through my mind and body. "What-if I play horrible?" "What-if I embarrass myself?" "What-if I singlehandedly lose the game?"

All of this what-ifing created a mind-body lockdown. The obsessive overthinking and fear of failure that I was experiencing generated wave after wave of physical symptomology, most notably: A racing heart, sweaty palms, clenched and tightened muscles, and some mild dizziness. "What-if I can't even play?"

A Nightmare in Real Time

I was doomed. I had sealed my fate. I lasted for five minutes into the first quarter. I turned the ball over four times, missed two jump shots and a layup, and committed two fouls. Not only did I feel lost and confused, but powerless to initiate any positive change. My coaches and teammates thought I was sick. Coach Finnegan left at halftime. I never heard from him again.

I did it. I unintentionally created and cultivated a guaranteed formula for failure. I focused on all that could go wrong. And it did!

Over the next few days I obsessed on "why" I had played so poorly and simultaneously worried "what-if" it happens again. It was really hard to let go of this negativity and fear of failure. I continued to play well most of the time but was prone to episodes of what-ifing, self-criticizing, and why-ning ("Why did I do that?"). I was allowing The Toxic Three of Poor Performance to prevent me from playing at my best and having fun on a consistent basis.

The Toxic Three of Poor Performance: Zone Blockers
(Symptoms and Anxieties)

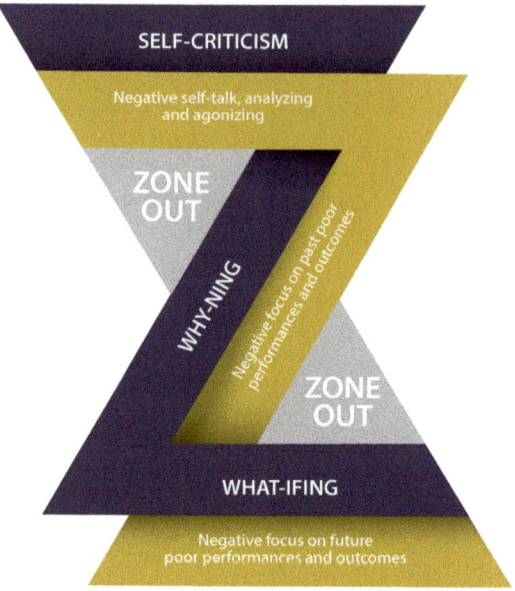

The Toxic Three:
1. Self-criticism (negative self-talk; analyzing and agonizing).

2. Why-ning (negative focus on past poor performances and outcomes). "Why did I do that?"

3. What-ifing (negative focus on future poor performances and outcomes). "What if I fail?"

While working with student-athletes at the elementary school, high school, and college levels, I have also worked extensively with professional athletes. Whether it's a little league baseball shortstop, a high school field hockey player, a college swimmer, or any athlete from any walk of life; I have been routinely peppered with toxic questions and negative expectations from student-athletes.

I have discovered that the most common questions are variations of "What-If I fail?" and "Why did I play that way?" The most common self-assessments are: "I am the worst," "I'll never make it," "I can't believe I choked," and so on. All of these questions are symptoms of anxiety that are born of the ultimate concern, "Where did my zone go?"

The Zone Lives Inside of You

Owen's reaction after experiencing a zone exercise during his first session was: "So Mr. Dowling, where did my zone go last year, and how can I find it this year?"

Owen's question was met with my response: "You just experienced a zone right here and now with 15 minutes of inner focus. You comfortably lost track of time and were really calm reviewing your love of baseball, the supportive people in your life, and the future success that awaits you this season. Your zone really does exist inside of you, specifically in your subconscious mind, the part of your mind that you just accessed, that only knows how to help you.

You don't know consciously how you walk, talk, read, catch a ball, breathe, write, or slide into home plate. I don't even know how I'm talking right now, how my hands are moving. I simply trust myself to talk and walk, to read and write. I just know that I know how to do these things. By the way, can you explain to me how you walked into the office from your car?" (I have yet to encounter someone who can answer this question with anything other than, "I just do it.")

I continued, "How about telling me how you swing the bat? It's interesting to know that you trusted yourself a long time ago when you were learning how to walk, yet now, today, you would never say, 'What-if I forget how to walk?' 'What-if I can't run when I wake up tomorrow?'

It's the self-criticism, the what-ifs, the whys, and the negative focus on the past, present, and future that keeps you from connecting with your zone. So, let's talk about how you just experienced your zone so easily and effectively."

I went on to emphasize for Owen how The Toxic Three (self-criticism, why-ning, what-ifing) are the most common ways people remain in performance slumps. Specifically, that it's not possible to play well if you are beating yourself up, focusing on past failures, and imagining all that will go wrong.

I said, "Owen, here's the deal: Overthinking and negativity will all but guarantee you will go 0 for 4 with a couple of strike outs. It's what causes you, and anyone else for that matter, to lose your zone, to zone-out."

ZONEfulness®

The Big Three of Peak Performance: Powerfully Calm Techniques

The Big Three:

1. Extreme Self-Support (internal strength).
1a. Support from family, friends, coaches, and teammates (external strength).

2. Personal History of Success (positive focus on past peak performances and outcomes). Magnifying the good!

3. Future Memories of Success (positive focus on future peak performances and outcomes).
   What-willing: "What-will it be like when I succeed?"

Owen was introduced to The Big Three of Peak Performance when I guided him into the 15 minute zone during his first session. He was able to comfortably explore his Personal History of Success; experience Future Memories of Success; and reconnect with the support he has received from family, friends, coaches, and teammates while focusing on his own capacity to support himself at a higher level.

How Zoning Out Triggers Zoning In

Session two began with a discussion of how the zone blockers, notably The Toxic Three, can be utilized as positive triggers to zone in and perform at your best. I explained, "Owen, whenever you find yourself what-ifing, worrying, or beating yourself up, make the problem the solution."

Owen looked at me quizzically as I continued, "Say, 'Thank you what-if, for reminding me, what-will it be like when I play well and hit the ball hard.' 'Thank you what-if, for reminding me to remember my love for the game and my Personal History of Success.' 'Thank you self-criticism, for reminding me to treat myself like I would a teammate or a good friend.'

So, you see, the zone blockers, the symptoms, can actually be used to your advantage. Symptoms make you zone out and play poorly. Now, they really can be incorporated as powerful reminders, to zone in. And remember, the symptoms that take you out of your zone live in your conscious mind, which is extremely small and limited. But your zone lives in your subconscious mind, the place where you can really trust and support yourself, that infinite space that creates calm, confidence, and peak performance."

Finally, I gave an example that I knew would be of personal significance to Owen, a lifelong Phillies fan. It went like this: "I want you to take a moment and remember the little league team you played on at the age of 12. Now, consider that the conscious mind that blocks your zone and creates anxiety is this team." (His team was the Mets.)

"Just imagine that your subconscious mind is a major league team, let's say the Phillies. Could the Mets, a bunch of 12-year-olds, ever beat the Philadelphia Phillies?" Owen rolled his eyes and laughed at this ridiculous question. "So, here's the best part of everything we've been talking about: Your subconscious mind, where your zone lives, is the Phillies, and your conscious mind, where the symptoms live, is the Mets.

The subconscious mind can't ever lose to the conscious mind and I know that you already know that the Phillies would never lose to a little league team. So, your zone is extraordinarily stronger than any worry, why, what-if, or self-criticism. And now these symptoms can trigger your zone!" Owen's comfortably curious look was becoming more and more hopeful.

No One Gets Rid of Anything

Clients frequently tell me that they want to "get rid of anxiety and negativity." The reality is that we always have the ability to be happy, sad, angry, afraid, confident, calm, content, enraged, overcome with laughter, frozen with surprise, and yes, anxious and negative. We are alive, vibrant, reactive, complicated individuals. However, we can learn to modulate and regulate our responses. Specifically, in the world of peak performance we can use symptoms to our advantage, as positive triggers, to reconnect with our zone.

My personal history with experiencing self-criticism and what-ifing, and in turn helping others to understand these negative reactions to our environment while providing the tools needed to work through them, doesn't mean that I'm not prone to flare-ups. These symptoms reverberated through me for many years, wreaking havoc with their unpredictability and toxic energy on and off the basketball court. They may still show themselves from time to time before a speaking engagement or during a workshop with a team.

These symptoms continue to live inside of me. But presently, they are microscopic. It's not possible to get rid of them completely. When these symptoms are provoked, I recognize the triggers, which allow me to launch into my inner dialogue: "Thank you, what-if, for reminding me what-will it be like when I succeed. Thank you, self-criticism, for reminding me to talk to myself like I would a good friend."

This inner dialogue dissolves the symptoms back to their microscopic resting place. I use the symptoms of anxiety and negativity as powerful reminders to support myself and to zone–in.

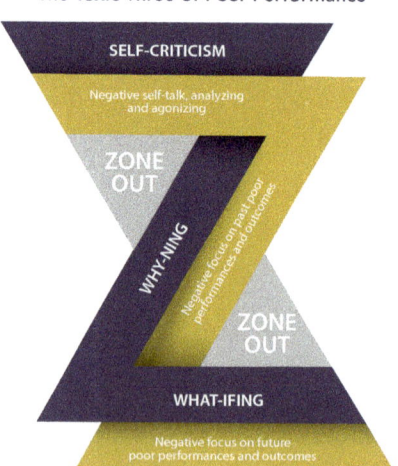

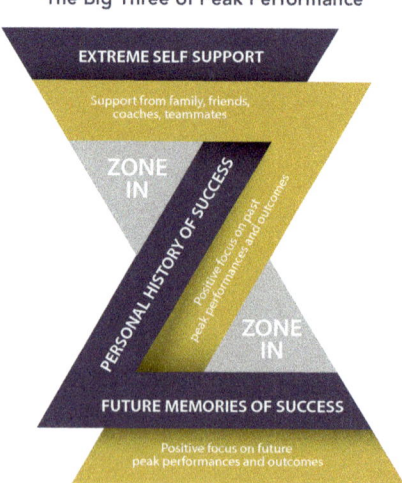

ZONEFULNESS®: A CASE STUDY
5TH INNING TRIUMPH

A major league baseball player who was mired in a most unusual slump was referred to me. As a first year starting pitcher he was unable to make it through the 5th inning of his first five starts of the season. He rapidly developed an irrational belief that he would never again make it through the 5th inning.

Interestingly, he pitched extremely well during the first four innings of each game he started. After being unable to survive the 5th in his first two starts he began to worry. Specifically, he began to "what-if" about not making it through this most troublesome inning. So, the five days he had to endure between starts became mentally excruciating.

He began obsessively engaging The Toxic Three zone blockers that guarantee poor performance. "What- if it happens again?" "What-if I get sent down to Triple-A?" "Why am I playing like this?" "I don't belong in the big leagues, I'll never make it, I'm a loser," played over and over in his conscious, overthinking mind. Unbelievably, he explained that he would actually calculate his earned run average (ERA) rising during the 5th inning. He would do this after surrendering runs, prior to the next batter stepping up to the plate.

Now, I already understood that anyone who makes it to "the show," the big leagues, is a world class athlete. Any major league baseball player is better than 99.9999% of the players in the world. So when he said to me at the outset of our session, "I don't know what you think you can do, I already know I'll never make it through the 5th inning," I was prepared.

I continued, "I have a question for you, but I don't want you to answer it until later in the session. Here goes: 'What's so special about the 5th inning?' I promise we'll come back to it."

I proceeded to inquire about his Personal History of Success, his ability to support himself and his teammates when having a difficult time, and about his Future Memories of Success. I was highlighting The Big Three techniques that create Peak Performance.

Personal History of Success:
Why-ning (asking, "Why did I play so poorly?") is used as a positive trigger to magnify your Personal History of Success.

I was curious about the road that brought him to the highest level of professional baseball. "So let's put the stress and pressure aside for just a moment and talk about pure baseball." I continued with the following questions, "When did you first realize you loved the game? Who were your primary supporters? What are your most meaningful memories of your life in baseball, from little league, and high school, on to the minor leagues?"

Over the next five minutes I learned a great deal about his passion for the game. He told me of "playing from the time I could barely walk with my brothers and dad; the smell of the glove oil I would use to break in a new mitt; the ping of the aluminum bat when I hit home runs; the sound of my mom's voice cheering me on; the awesome feeling of getting drafted; the party we had when I signed my first contract," and on and on he went.

I could feel his energy heightening as he reconnected with and detailed his Personal History of Success in baseball. So I said, "Can you tell me about a time, from little league to the present, excluding your past five major league starts, that you did NOT make it through the 5th inning?" I fully anticipated that he would remember a few times when he was off his game and was taken out prior to the 5th inning. He looked up for a minute and reviewed his career as a pitcher and realized that he could not, amazingly, remember a single time he was removed from a game, on any level, before this season. "So what's so special about the 5th inning? Don't answer that yet."

Extreme Self-Support:
Self-criticizing is used as a positive trigger
to become Extremely Self-Supportive.

I then wondered aloud if he had a close friend on the team. After learning that he is extremely close with a fellow pitcher, I asked him how he would support his buddy if the roles were reversed, if he were pitching very well and his friend was convinced that he would never again see the start of the sixth inning. He emphatically responded that he would tell his friend, "You belong here! You destroy hitters! You are the man! I wish I had the nasty stuff you have! I believe in you!"

I commented, "Imagine if you took 20% of the genuine, heartfelt support you have for your friend and applied it to yourself. And, by the way, would you ever advise another pitcher in a slump to beat himself down, to focus on future failure, and, in what universe would you recommend that he calculate his ERA going up while he was still in the game pitching?" I detected a slight smile and a nod of the head.

Future Memories of Success:

What-ifing (What if I fail?) is used as a positive trigger to begin What-willing (What-will it be like when I succeed?).

I then posed a series of pointed questions, "What-will it be like when every pitch is the first pitch and every inning the first inning? Isn't every pitch an opportunity to be extremely confident and intense? And, please help me understand what's so special about the 5th inning? I noticed his smile became a bit wider and his head continued nodding in agreement.

He sat upright in his chair and said, "What IS the big deal about the 5th inning? It's just another inning." We then discussed the philosophy of allowing every pitch to simply be the next pitch, the first pitch. I went on, "Every pitch can be a positive trigger to trust your ability, to really zone in, to be fiercely focused . . . and, by the way, my personal favorite technique is to imagine Future Memories of Success. And you can do that on the mound, seeing and experiencing success right before throwing the pitch, believing that in just a split second you will be achieving your goal. And then you do it again, and again, and again."

Peak Performance Zone:

This guided zone exercise allows The Big Three (Personal History of Success, Extreme Self-Support, Future Memories of Success) to become your go-to tools that enable intense focus and maximum achievement. Zone exercises in the office and at home serve to dismantle the symptoms that prevent you from accessing and maintaining your real-time performance zone in your sport.

As he sat comfortably in his chair I continued, "Close your eyes and take five very slow, very deep breaths. A nice way to really absorb yourself is to stare at the inside of your eyes, experiencing the unique light, the colors . . . and I know that your conscious mind may have certain doubts about this process, this exercise, but I also know from my experience that your subconscious mind is already creating and generating sensations of comfort and confidence, visions of your best self really competing, succeeding, and believing in your talents and abilities.

So, why not forget all about trying, and transport yourself back in time, like a bodiless mind, enjoying the process of reviewing your own personal history of playing ball . . . experiencing the sights and sounds of dominating on the mound, the sensations of lightness . . . the smell of the freshly cut grass, the powerfully calm confidence that flowed through you and remains within you."

I continued guiding him back through his Personal History of Success for five minutes, helping him to reconnect with memories of not only playing great but of loving to play.

The final ten minutes of the guided zone magnified the tools of Extreme Self-Support and Future Memories of Success.

The outcome:

The rookie pitcher went on to pitch four complete games throughout the remainder of the season. He routinely pitched beyond the 5th inning. The start after his ZONEfulness® session he pitched seven innings, gave up two runs, and earned his first major league victory. He was quoted after the game saying, "It's really about my mental focus. I just tried to take one pitch at a time and do my very best."

The Baby Zone

The zone is the second most natural thing people do next to breathing. We first experience our zone the moment we are born. Pay attention to babies, they intuitively go into profoundly deep zones. It is how they learn. Babies absorb themselves in everything. They stare down mom, the dog, and the paintings on the wall. They absorb themselves in music and deeply focus on new and familiar voices, they are constantly zoning in to the stimuli all around them.

The baby zone is where it all starts. As children grow the zone continues to expand to enable them to achieve more advanced learnings. For example, learning to walk is a daunting, difficult undertaking. Babies will stumble and fall countless times prior to taking that elusive first step yet never consider discontinuing the quest to walk.

History has never known a baby that thinks, "You know, I just really can't do this. What is wrong with me? What-if I never learn to walk? I'll never have any friends. I'll be stuck like this forever!" The child's naturalistic, meditative zone state creates an unwavering belief that walking is right around the corner.

Whether it's learning to read and write, throw and catch, or swim in the pool (to name just a few of the countless things we learn when intensely focused), the zone remains a huge part of each person throughout life.

In order to learn, to achieve goals and rise to the next level, you need to access your natural capacity to trust yourself. Self-trust is inherent in the zone. It helps to dissolve doubt, worry, fear, and the myriad of symptoms that serve as zone blockers. Trust is a hallmark of ZONEfulness®. So, your zone has been with you all along. It is readily available to you any time, all the time. Walk on.

Types of Zone Exercises

Owen's third session began with a discussion of the different types of zones, other than the guided, eyes closed, deeply focused zone he experienced in session one. I reviewed the zones and reiterated that not only would we be practicing them in the office but that he would have the opportunity to develop an expertise by practicing at home, in school, in the weight room, during training and games, anywhere.

Zone exercises include:

I. Guided zones
    A. Eyes closed zone (3+ minutes)
    B. Eyes open zone (3+ minutes)
    C. Power zone (1 to 3 minutes)
II. Self-zones
    A. Eyes closed zone (3+ minutes)
    B. Eyes open zone (3+ minutes)
    C. Power zone (1 to 3 minutes)
    D. Personal highlight zone (1 to 5+ minutes)

Eyes closed, as well as eyes open zones, can be recorded in session and listened to at home. They will likely vary in length. Zone recordings typically range from 3 to 15 minutes. Optimally, recordings of different lengths are provided to familiarize student-athletes with zone states. This will enable a more seamless transition to real-time practice and game competition.

Recordings are valuable in that they promote confidence when creating self-zones (zones that are self-produced outside of the office, not facilitated by a guide or a recording). After using self-zones for a period of time, they become second nature and are extremely valuable to peak performance.

The 1 to 3 minute power zone is a brief self-zone. Student-athletes who routinely engage in power zones a few times a day find that they can rapidly develop a mastery of accessing and maintaining their zone in practice and games. The brief power zone is simply five very slow, deep breaths (breathing in through the nose and out through the mouth), with eyes open or closed, while focusing on your Personal History of Success, Extreme Self-Support, or Future Memories of Success; or any combination of The Big Three.

The personal highlight film zone is an eyes open zone that is achieved by watching a video on your laptop, iPad, or smartphone, of your best performance(s). This zone can range from 1 to 5+ minutes and is, of course, done with your eyes open. It is best experienced by taking five slow, deep breaths prior to hitting play. Then you can really absorb yourself into the sights, sounds, and feelings of playing at your best.

III. Anchor zones

Anchors are sensory in nature. They are positive triggers that are experienced visually, auditorily, and kinesthetically (physically). Anchors can greatly enhance focus, confidence, and performance.

Anchor zones are experienced during the physical practice of your sport. Examples include:

- Visual anchors: The golfer who, upon standing over the ball, creates an intense tunnel vision. This intensity magnifies performance.

  The lacrosse player who locks her gaze on her stick and remembers her personal goal to "leave everything on the field."

  The sprinter who only sees the finish line tape and feels as if he's running alone through an aerodynamic channel.

- Auditory anchors: The softball player who listens intently to the sound of her own supportive voice prior to stepping into the batter's box. Her mantra, "Trust your swing" creates an expectation of success.

- The sound of her teammates cheering throughout her at-bat is another auditory anchor that focuses her attention on each pitch.

- The cross-country runner who listens to "the nature concert all around me." This personalized soundtrack creates a consistent flow and pace.

- Kinesthetic or physical anchors: The basketball player who pulls lightly on her jersey at the foul line is cued to zone in during her pre-shot routine.

- The ice hockey player who clenches and unclenches his fists inside his gloves before each face-off remembers his resolve to play hard.

- The soccer player who taps his foot two times prior to striking the penalty kick is locked on to his target.

Anchors are as varied as you are imaginative. The practice of zone exercises to follow will encourage you to create anchors and rapidly master your anchor zone.

The Eyes Have It

Midway through his third session Owen engaged in an eyes open, alert zone exercise. I suggested that he stare intently at the gold handles on the cabinet directly across from him. As he focused his attention on the handles, he took five very slow, very deep breaths, in the manner he experienced during his first session when he was guided into an eyes closed zone.

"Owen, as you focus your gaze on the handles you can begin to experience, in your own way, a tunnel vision . . . or perhaps it is more of a comfortable fuzziness. You can be really curious as you zone in on the handles. And I know you've had the experience on countless occasions of stepping into the batter's box—and you can, right now, review your most memorable at-bats. Did you pick up the ball the moment it left the pitcher's fingertips or was it like the ball was suddenly the size of a grapefruit? I'm wondering how that tunnel vision, that locked-in gaze felt."

I continued, "Was there an extreme confidence, a gut feeling that you would rip a double, a homer? Now, as you continue to absorb yourself on the handles, you can know, really know, that your zone, your confidence, your ability to believe, to really achieve, is available right now, just like it was back then, as it will be this season, during each at-bat."

Owen kept his eyes open for the first seven minutes of this guided zone before closing them for the final eight. Afterward, Owen expressed his energy in words: "Wow! That was unreal. I really like the eyes open beginning, it was just like staring through a tunnel. It's like I'm at the plate, ready to wail on the pitch." Neither of us knew, at that moment in time, just what his potential could be. We would soon find out.

4 Techniques to Access and Master Your Zone

ZONE EXERCISE:

HOW TO ACCESS AND MAINTAIN YOUR PEAK PERFORMANCE ZONE

This zone exercise can be experienced by going to ZONEfulness.com and clicking on the audio file, **Guided Zone: How to Access and Maintain Your Peak Performance Zone**. To really benefit and enjoy the recording it is crucial to not only listen to the audio but to EXPERIENCE it. So, prior to hitting play, close your eyes and take five very deep, very slow breaths. After the guided zone begins, allow yourself to simply experience and explore. In other words, have some fun and just go with the flow. It's not even possible to do it wrong, so just be curious as you follow along.

Strong recommendation: After listening to the guided zone, take a couple of minutes and experience it as a self-zone. Simply follow the four steps listed below. Practicing your self-zone will enable you to more easily and effectively generate peak performance in real-time competition. This zone exercise is a nice warm-up for the following chapters that will guide you through The Big Three of Peak Performance.

Create Your Peak Performance Self Zone
1. Close your eyes and take five very slow, very deep breaths. Remember to breathe in through your nose and out your mouth.

2. Transport yourself back in time to your Personal History of Success. Revivify and magnify the sights, sounds, and feelings of your best moments and experiences in your sport.

3. Feel the power of Extreme Self-Support. Begin by hearing the sound of your own voice supporting friends, family, and teammates and reconnect with the times you have been supported by coaches, teammates, family, and friends.

4. Transport yourself into Future Memories of Success. Imagine yourself playing at your very best. Experience the focus and confidence of being zoned in.

ZONEfulness®

4 Techniques to Access and Master Your Zone

PART TWO

ZONEfulness®

The Big Three of Peak Performance & A Final Fourth Technique

ZONEfulness®

4 Techniques to Access and Master Your Zone

CHAPTER FIVE

MAGNIFY THE GOOD

TECHNIQUE #1: PERSONAL HISTORY OF SUCCESS

"Somewhere behind the athlete you've become and the hours of practice and the coaches who have pushed you is a little girl who fell in love with the game and never looked back. Play for her."
— Mia Hamm, National Hall of Fame Soccer Player,
2004 Olympic Gold Medalist

ZONEfulness®: A CASE STUDY
THE LACROSSE PLAYER

A high school lacrosse player was referred to me in the hope of breaking out of a performance slump. Jill, now a junior, wasn't just any player. She was extraordinary. As a sophomore, she was her team's leading scorer, chosen MVP, selected to first team all-league, and even made the all-state team.

When Jill sat across from me six games into the season she looked sad and defeated. She began to cry as she explained, "I haven't scored in the last four games. I just want to quit. Those girls won't leave me alone."

As Jill settled into the session she detailed the exact nature of her problem. On the surface it appeared that she had become a shell of her former tenacious, aggressive, goal scoring self. She had stopped shooting and began forcing passes to teammates. I learned that the head coach had grown so frustrated imploring Jill to shoot that she was left with no choice but to bench her.

It became clear to me that Jill was being emotionally bullied by some of her teammates. They brutally attacked her with their words. In essence, they labeled her as selfish while mistakenly believing that she thought she was better than everyone else. The head coach expected Jill to just "tough it out."

Jill is a good person. She is caring and compassionate, while also being very sensitive. She became so overwhelmed with the harassment that she shut down emotionally. Jill lost her edge on the field. She began to play poorly to prove she was just another player. She attempted to fit in by not playing up to her potential. She was unintentionally giving her emotional and physical power away.

At the time of our first session Jill was fully immersed in The Toxic Three of Poor Performance. "Why are they so mean to me?" "Why can't I play well?" "What-If they don't accept me?" "I don't think I can play anymore!"

I learned from Jill that she came from a close-knit family and had good friends on and off the team. She told me she had always loved and dedicated herself to lacrosse but now "couldn't stand playing anymore." I remember feeling the sadness and desperation that flowed from her as she slumped down in her chair.

But there was something more happening beneath the surface. I sensed her competitive spirit was alive and well but being blocked. I wanted to help Jill unleash her passion for lacrosse and fully support herself.

"So Jill, I want to ask you to do something. For the next few minutes I'd like to put all of this difficult stuff aside and shift gears. Do you know how to take a deep breath?

After a 90 second deep breathing warm-up I asked Jill to keep her eyes closed and to begin breathing easily and naturally. "Now I'm going to ask you some questions and I want you to really take your time before answering.

When did you first know that you loved lacrosse?

I continued, "Allow yourself to pay attention to your rhythmic breathing, the shades of light on the inside of your eyes, and on the feeling of stillness that you've developed over the last couple of minutes. As you absorb yourself into these feelings of comfort you can really enjoy remembering all the fun you've had playing lacrosse. Take your time and experience the sights, sounds, the sensations and feelings of just playing for fun from the time you were a little girl, through grade school, all the way to high school . . . "

And there it was. What a smile! Jill seemed to glow as she began to tell me about her lifetime of loving lacrosse. She detailed receiving a stick as a "five or six year old on Christmas morning." She spoke happily of summer camps and told me a funny story about her first coach.

"When did you know you were the best player on most of the teams you've played on and how did it feel?"

Hesitantly, Jill stated, "I guess I just knew, I think I just loved it more than anyone else."

"Tell me about a memorable game or games when you played amazingly. And I want to encourage you to just enjoy the feelings as you remember your history of playing well, of being in the zone. You can give yourself permission to let go of worrying that you are bragging when you tell me about your experiences. So, just let it flow."

It was clear that Jill was comfortably in a zone as she answered this question. Her smile continued as she spoke of a number of games where she, incredibly, scored ten or more goals; championship games when she was in grade school and junior high; times when her picture was in the newspaper and the day she was interviewed by the local TV news station.

"Tell me about a time before this season that you didn't give 100% of yourself in a lacrosse game?"

Jill stated, "I've always played as hard as I can play."

"Now take about a minute or two or three of real clock time and really review your personal history of always playing incredibly hard." Jill nodded as two minutes went by in silence.

"That's right. Now is just the time to magnify the sights, sounds, and feelings of playing with intensity and fierce focus. You can really enjoy experiencing your own personal highlight film of scoring goals and playing great. Finally, you can take a bit more time and give yourself a hand for being so open to exploring and reconnecting with your genuine love and respect for the game of lacrosse. You can give yourself even more support for having had the desire and courage to come here today.

Now, take five slightly deeper breaths and, whenever you are ready, open your eyes and feel the calm. That's right, taking your time."

As Jill opened her eyes her smile grew wider. Before giving her a few homework assignments I said, "Jill, I'm wondering how much you are going to enjoy reconnecting with loving to play the game you love."

Jill's homework assignments were:
1. Be really respectful to lacrosse, make up to lacrosse by being fiercely focused and by having fun playing.

2. Be overwhelmingly nice to yourself while reviewing your Personal History of Success for 1 to 3 minutes a day.

3. Use any distraction as a reminder to play your best.

I met with Jill five times over the next month. We never really talked that much about lacrosse. We talked a great deal about how people who are respected and valued by others seem to know how to speak their mind. Jill was beginning to understand that communicating genuinely and honestly creates positive energy. She was learning the value of expressing herself, regardless of the subject matter. Her best self was taking charge.

I learned in our second session that Jill had discussed a plan of action with her parents. They decided Jill would approach the girls who were bullying her and assertively tell them to stop. Jill did just that. Unfortunately, after she confronted them they continued their bullying. This time, however, she had a new strategy designed to take her power back.

4 Techniques to Access and Master Your Zone

Over the next few weeks she went on a scoring binge. The team went on a winning streak. She began to receive letters of interest from Division I college lacrosse programs. She used the harassment as a reminder to magnify the good, specifically, her Personal History of Success. She told me, "They didn't even know they were motivating me so much."

I enjoy talking with Jill on occasion these days. I'll hear from her a time or two a year when she wants to process a challenge or overcome an obstacle in her life. Oh, by the way, she earned a scholarship to play lacrosse at a Division I college. She is playing very well and working toward her degree in education. We rarely talk about lacrosse.

Positive Psychology

I'm extremely interested in what's right with people. I enjoy learning about their past and present achievements while discussing future possibilities and potentials.

Traditional psychological therapy is enamored with figuring out the "why" and labeling people with a diagnosis. It is heavily laden with analysis, testing, and much too frequently reliant on medication. It often is a cumbersome, boring experience that encourages people to believe that they are flawed and in need of long-term therapy.

Positive psychology (specifically solution-oriented and strategic therapy) focuses on the unique strengths of each individual. ZONEfulness® is a strength-based, future-focused model that empowers student-athletes to access the answers and abilities that they already possess. The peak performance zone that exists inside of each person is loaded with solutions and creative strategies.

Magnifying the past, present, and future good is the foundation of peak performance psychology. Solution-oriented questions and strategic task assignments will be highlighted in the ZONEfulness® techniques to follow.

Solution-Oriented Questions: Personal History of Success

I've asked the following questions of student-athletes over the years to assist them in reconnecting with their Personal History of Success.

- "Tell me about a time you played soccer with extreme confidence?"
- "What would you consider to be the best round of golf you ever played?"
- "When did you realize you loved throwing the shot put?"
- "When did you know that the backstroke would be your best event?"
- "How would your favorite coach describe your strengths as a hockey player?"
- "What individual honors have you achieved as a sprinter? What team honors?"

- "How do you feel about yourself after a huge workout in the weight room in preparation for football camp?"

- "What do you enjoy doing after a Friday night hoop victory?"

- "Tell me about your pre-race ritual and how you focus your attention to compete?"

Strategic Assignments: Personal History of Success

I've given the following homework assignments to student-athletes to enable them to experience their Personal History of Success.

- "I want you to do a 3 minute or more self-zone tonight focusing on your performance last week when you scored 15 points and had 8 assists. Magnify the feelings, flow, and confidence that you experienced."

- "After listening to your zone recording tonight after dinner, go out back and throw ten fastballs to your dad."

- "Watch your personal highlight film on your laptop tonight. Afterwards, take five deep breaths and enjoy imagining your team winning the lacrosse championship this weekend."

- "Before next session, go to your little brother's soccer game and intently watch the kids who are zoned-in and playing intensely. I'll look forward to hearing what you learned."

- "I know you are leaving campus for a few days and traveling home for Thanksgiving break. While you are home slowly review your dad's scrapbook. Enjoy all of the photos, the newspaper clippings, and the memories. Let yourself reconnect with your history of loving to play tennis and of being a great tennis player. Bring the feelings of confidence and trust in yourself back to campus on Sunday."

The number of solution-oriented questions and strategic assignments are limitless. They are designed based on the unique history and future potential of each student-athlete I train.

ZONEfulness®: A CASE STUDY
"I'M WATCHING THE VIDEOS ALL THE TIME."

A senior co-captain of a very good Division I baseball team contacted me in a state of desperation. He explained over the phone, "I really need help. I'm 2 for 21 in our first 6 games. I'm supposed to be one of our best hitters. Do you have any openings tomorrow morning?"

When Bill arrived to my office at 8:15 the next morning he shook my hand, sat down and said, "I don't know why I can't hit this year. Why can't I figure out what's wrong? I'm watching the videos all the time."

I was compelled to ask him more about what video footage he was watching. Instead, I simply said, "Bill, I can feel your sense of urgency, your motivation to be the player you know you can be. So, before we discuss the videos you are watching and your inability to figure things out, tell me about your history of playing well. I'm curious, how did you play last season as a junior?"

Bill responded, "That's the thing. I was second team all-conference. I led the team in home runs and my batting average was .341. So, why can't I hit this year?"

I asked him, "So, what did that zone feel like last season?" "I was in complete control," he replied. "I just saw the pitch and hit it, usually hard."

"O.k.," I said. "Tell me more, and feel free to take your time, about your history of playing ball. Specifically, when did you know you loved to play? What are some of your best performances? If you were putting together your personal highlight film, going back to little league, what would be included in the video?"

Over the next ten minutes Bill detailed his extraordinary love of baseball. He told me about winning back-to-back little league championships in his home town; being named the best athlete in his high school; hitting a home run in an all-star game; his "amazing" three years at his current college. He took great pride in being voted team captain in this, his senior year.

"That is some impressive Personal History of Success. I'm sensing it felt good to reconnect with those memories of being in the zone and just letting it flow?" Bill responded, "Oh yeah, just talking about it chills me out."

We then spent some time talking about the zone, self-support versus self-criticism, and other principles of ZONEfulness®. I felt that Bill was connecting with the discussion and had shifted his focus from negativity to curiosity.

"So, I've been waiting to ask you an extremely important question." I purposely paused to get Bill's full attention. I leaned in and focused directly on him. "Please tell me what videos you've been watching throughout your hitting slump."

Looking a bit confused, Bill said, "What do you mean? I'm breaking down my at-bats from the start of the season trying to straighten things out."

Now smiling, I volleyed back to Bill. "You're doing what? Breaking down your at-bats from this season? You're analyzing the strikeouts; the weak ground balls? You're watching yourself fail over and over and over again? That must be exhausting!"

The remainder of the session consisted of a 15 minute Personal History of Success zone exercise. I guided Bill to step back into the sights, sounds, feelings, and sensations of his most confident, effective performances.

His homework was to watch the videos of his all-conference season from the previous year. I enthusiastically told him: "Go home tonight and watch the complete highlight reel from your junior year. Fully absorb yourself in your swing; your homerun trot; the victories; anything and everything that created and generated confidence. Enjoy reconnecting with your peak performance zone."

Just about 12 hours after our session I received a phone call. It was Bill.
"Thanks for answering the phone this late. I just had to call to thank you for today's session. I watched the videos and I can't tell you how good I feel. I'm pumped for my game tomorrow!"

He continued, "I have to tell you that my girlfriend and I were laughing hysterically when I told her how you asked me what videos I was watching. We actually had a pretty cool discussion about being positive and focusing on what's good."

I felt Bill's sense of relief and his growing confidence as the conversation continued. "By the way, you said something, I think, about future memoires? Can I come in the same time tomorrow morning and do a zone about the rest of the season? I'm starting to get really excited!"

Bill came in the next morning and enjoyed his Future Memories of Success zone, which we recorded. He went 3 for 4 later that day with 2 doubles and 2 runs batted in.

He was once again the team leader in home runs and surpassed his junior year batting average by hitting .357. He was named second team all-conference.

The Toxic Three versus The Big Three

Round 1: Why-ning versus Personal History of Success

Why-ning is a cutthroat, ferocious member of The Toxic Three of Poor Performance. A zone buster of epic proportions, why-ning takes great pride in creating why-ners (whiners.) "Why did I make that pass? Why did I miss the open net? Why is everyone against me? Why can't I be a starter?"

Why-ning prevents ZONEfulness®. It blocks you from your zone. It's not possible to feel the flow of confidence that your zone provides if you are always asking "why?"

"Why" is a symptom that lives in your conscious, overthinking mind. The zone lives in your subconscious mind. Remember, your subconscious mind is infinitely more powerful than your conscious mind. And I know that you are beginning to understand that your zone lives inside of you and is ready, willing, and extraordinarily capable of crushing any symptom.

Brief dream sequence: *Take a moment and imagine a soccer team composed of 10-year-old girls. The girls on this team are considered the best players in the United States in their age group.*

Take another moment and imagine that a contract has been signed committing this team of all-star 10-year-olds to play Manchester United (arguably the world's best soccer team comprised of men in their 20s and 30s) at Wembly Stadium in front of 90,000 fans.

Now, close your eyes and imagine this ridiculous game being played!

End dream sequence. Begin reality check. Your zone is Manchester United. Your symptoms are the 10-year-old girls. Your zone wants to play in the game. Let it in. Your symptoms simply can't compete against your zone

Using Why-ning to Your Advantage – Part 1

A foundational component of positive, solution-oriented psychology is that the problem becomes the solution. The problem, asking why, can be used as a powerful trigger to create a solution.

Whenever you notice that you are why-ning, say, "Thank you why, for reminding me to remember my Personal History of Success. Thank you why, for triggering me to remember the two goals I scored in last year's playoff game."

The why reminds you to magnify what's not only good, but really great, about your personal history of playing your sport.

Why-ning, like any symptom, is trying to throw you off your game. It acts like a con-man trying to convince you to analyze and overthink.

Analysis will indeed produce paralysis. Or at a minimum, it will block you from your performance zone.

So, pay attention to the "whys." When you thank the why for reminding you to validate your history of playing well it may initially feel awkward. So have some fun with it. Be sarcastic when you say, "Thank you why, for reminding me to trust myself and kick some butt today." Or, depending on your mood, you may choose to say, "Bleep you why, for triggering my passion for playing the game I love."

The why symptom knows it can't compete with your zone. It will, however, continue to attempt to fight with you. So don't fight, laugh at the pathetic why.

Remember, no one gets rid of anything. We are all prone to why-ning, self-criticizing, and what-ifing at any time. The Toxic Three can appear even after you have developed a mastery of turning symptoms into solutions.

But now you know what to do! Turn the why into a reminder that you really can remember your unique history of loving to play and of playing well.

This ZONEfulness® technique is extraordinarily effective when preparing yourself mentally to compete in your sport. While in the heat of battle, however, there just isn't any time to do a 1 minute power zone and review your Personal History of Success.

So, when confronted with a why after making a mistake in real-time competition, use it to instantaneously focus your attention and anticipate success.

Using Why-ning to Your Advantage – Part 2

Another effective characteristic of solution-oriented therapy and positive psychology is the deceptively simple, profoundly effective strategy of doing things differently.

Whenever you experience the why symptom use it as a reminder to do something different. Just do anything different.

For example, if you start asking yourself why you threw an interception or missed an easy putt, say, "Thank you why, for reminding me to use my left hand when I brush my teeth. Thank you why, for triggering me to do ten pushups. Bleep you why, for reminding me to take five deep breaths. Thank you why, for reminding me to listen to my zone recording. Thank you why, for cueing me to call my boyfriend and sing to him."

By doing things differently you are shifting out of the problematic pattern of overthinking. Remember, the opposite of thinking is DOING.

ZONEfulness®: A CASE STUDY
CARL: WHY-NING

A wide receiver on a Division I college football team complained of "constant negative thinking."

I can't prove it but Carl may have set the world record for why questions in the first ten minutes of our session. When he finally took a breath I said, "Why ask why?" To which Carl said, "What do you mean?"

We will discuss the great work Carl did in his ZONEfulness® training as the book progresses. But for now, let's enjoy the wonderfully creative cure he discovered for his why-ning habit.

One of Carl's homework assignments was to pay attention to how many times a day he asked himself why he didn't catch the pass or why he didn't do this or why he didn't do that.

Next, he was to use the why to his advantage anytime he found himself why-ning and say, "Thank you why, for reminding me to do something different."
Carl asked me what he was supposed to do different. I replied, "I don't know. Do anything you want."

Our second session began with Carl telling me what he started doing after asking why. He said, "Right after our session I kept asking myself why you didn't tell me what to do differently. When I noticed I was asking why, I decided to pick up my guitar and play. And it was really funny because I then wondered why I chose playing my guitar as the thing I would do differently.

Anyway, in the last week I must have played my guitar at least 25 times. But only about 10 were because I asked why. I love the guitar and didn't realize how much I missed playing. It really helps me relax and focus.

I even started asking 'Why ask why?'"

4th Sport Psychology Session with Owen, March, 2013

Owen: "When can we do the zone? I'm getting great at going really fast into it. I've been listening to the recordings we've made and doing the one minute power zone like, five times a day.

Can you believe in my first session that I asked you where my zone went? I can't wait for the season to start."

With a trip to Florida and the first game of the season only two days away, Owen was psyched up to start playing games for real.

I suggested that he once again fixate his attention on the gold handles across the room.

The session began with the two of us discussing how the peak performance zone is easily accessible when listening to a recording, doing a power zone, and playing in a game.

Owen said, "I've been practicing tunneling my vision on the ball as it comes out of the pitcher's hand. What's that again, the anchor?"

"Exactly," I said, "that's your real-time visual anchor. It's just like the eyes open zone you did here."

Owen, "Yeah, I can really see the ball better. I pick up the spin a lot easier."

"Yes! That's your zone. You are locking in and trusting yourself."

I went on to emphasize for Owen that practicing his zone off the field was enabling him to more easily experience it on the field. "The last few weeks of mental focus training are now officially part of your Personal History of Success," I continued. "Now you can look forward to mastering your ability to zone in anytime."

Owen: "I know. I want to get to where I don't think about anything. I just want go with the flow. I will definitely be listening to my zone recording on the plane to Florida tomorrow!"

The remainder of the session consisted of a Personal History of Success zone exercise. Owen wanted to begin the experience in an eyes open zone and see how long he could keep them open."

I guided him to stare across the room and focus his attention on the gold handles.

I suggested that he, "Really enjoy remembering how, less than a month ago, you didn't really know that your zone lived inside of you. And now, you do know that you have created, really generated, a major shift. An awesome shift that can allow you to believe in your ability to really achieve.

You can take an entire minute of real clock time to magnify this shift. You can remember your first zone exercise from here in the office; you can experience the energy, the hope, and the curiosity that you had then, just as if it were now. That's right!"

I continued, "You can feel the freedom to reconnect with how it felt to experience the zone recordings; how easily the power zones intensified your focus.

You can really appreciate what you've accomplished and bring all of those confident, flowing feelings into the present, into the now, feeling the power of now. That's right!"

I could see Owen was really getting it.

"Your Personal History of Success is going to Florida with you. It's yours. It's part of your flow. So you can really let go . . . turn on that fastball, wait on the curve . . . enjoy creating new memories, always adding more to your Personal History of Success file."

During the remainder of the zone exercise I had Owen close his eyes and fully absorb himself into the stillness, the mindfulness of his new and enhanced perspective regarding his past and present success.

He commented before leaving the office, "I'm not totally sure why, but I really can't wait to hit."

The Power of Positive Memories
Cole Hamels versus The Cincinnati Reds and Great American Ball Park

June 7, 2014

Cole Hamels pitched 7 and 2/3 innings with 7 strikeouts as the Philadelphia Phillies defeated the Cincinnati Reds 8-0 at Cincinnati's Great American Ball Park. Hamels, the 2008 National League Championship Series and World Series Most Valuable Player, is the ace of the Phillies pitching staff.

Not only is Hamels undefeated when pitching in Cincinnati, but he has most impressively experienced unprecedented success and achieved two major personal milestones there against the Reds.

May 12, 2006
Phillies 8, Reds 4

In his major league debut at Great American Ballpark Cole Hamels pitched five shutout innings while surrendering only one hit and striking out seven batters.

October 10, 2010
Phillies 2, Reds 0

Cole Hamels threw a complete game shutout with nine strikeouts and no walks as the Phillies eliminated the Reds from the postseason in this divisional playoff closeout game at Great American Ballpark.

Hamels' Career Statistics versus The Reds

The Phillies are 13-0 from 2006 – 2014 when Cole Hamels starts against the Reds.

Hamels' individual stats include:
Games started: 13
Wins: 10
Losses: 0
No decisions: 3
Complete games: 2
Strikeouts: 81
Walks: 27
ERA: 1.15
Reds batting average against Hamels: .170

June 7, 2014

Following his commanding performance, Hamels spoke to the media during the postgame press conference.

"Anytime I'm here (at Great American Ballpark) going up against that team, it's what I associate, those positive memories . . . that jump start me. When I face them, when I'm here . . . I'm in a better zone."

Phillies manager, Ryne Sandberg, contributed to the press conference, "That's (playing against the Reds at Great American Ballpark) probably what he feeds off of . . . the positive thoughts and memories."

I'm rather certain Cole Hamels would enjoy creating a personal history of performing at Great American Ballpark zone before pitching in New York, Los Angeles, Chicago, at home in Philadelphia, or anywhere at all.

How rapidly would he break out of a slump by revivifying his perfect record against the Reds?

You can embrace your Personal History of Success! The most meaningful moments of your past can help you to create a powerfully confident present.

ZONE EXERCISES:
PERSONAL HISTORY OF SUCCESS

Guided Zone

You can participate in this zone exercise by going to ZONEfulness.com and clicking on the audio file, **Guided Zone: Personal History of Success.**

Remember to fully experience the zone, not just listen to the recording. Follow along with my voice and enjoy reconnecting with your unique Personal History of Success.

Self-Zone

After listening to the recording, take at least three minutes and go into a self-zone. It's not necessary to do it right away but make sure you practice going into your self-zone without the recording. Simply take five very slow, very deep breaths and review the sights, sounds, and feelings associated with your Personal History of Success.

You can experiment with doing the guided and self-zones with your eyes open for some or all of the experience. Find out what works best for you.

Power Zone

Practice your power zone. It takes only 1 to 3 minutes. Before school, at lunch, really anytime, taking even just one minute will greatly enhance your ability to tap into your zone while practicing or playing in a real-time competition.

Power zones can also be accessed with your eyes opened or closed.

Anchor Zones

When practicing your sport, create an anchor. It can be visual, auditory, kinesthetic or any combination of the three.

Owen very rapidly developed a skill for creating a tunnel vision as the ball came out of the pitcher's hand during batting practice and in games. This visual anchor allowed him to intensify his focus and build his Personal History of Success.

See page 33 for more examples of anchors.

Personal Highlight Film Zone

Watch the videos. The videos of your best swing; your best time; or your best shot, save, or tackle; your best putt; your best check; your best pass or catch. Watch all of your highlights on your smartphone or PC.

Take 1 to 5+ minutes and absorb yourself in your personal highlight film zone. Ideally, you should take five slow, deep breaths, in through the nose and out through the mouth prior to hitting play.

If you do not have any highlights recorded, that's o.k. Simply get a teammate, friend, coach, or family member to record you practicing or competing.

Most importantly, enjoy watching yourself playing at your best!

4 Techniques to Access and Master Your Zone

CHAPTER SIX
LOVE AND PEACE WITH YOURSELF---OR ELSE!

TECHNIQUE #2: EXTREME SELF-SUPPORT (INTERNAL STRENGTH) SUPPORT FROM FAMILY, FRIENDS, COACHES, AND TEAMMATES (EXTERNAL STRENGTH)

"Make sure your worst enemy doesn't live between your ears."
— Laird Hamilton, Champion Big Wave Surfer

ZONEfulness®: A CASE STUDY
THE NEXT SHOT IS THE FIRST SHOT
An Ivy Dream

In October, 2009 I was invited to present a sport psychology, peak performance training program to the Cornell University men's basketball team by head coach Steve Donahue. Many years earlier, coach Donahue invited me to work with the University of Pennsylvania basketball team when he was just beginning his career as an assistant coach.

I soon learned The Big Red of Cornell was not your typical Ivy League team.

Princeton and Penn had held a stranglehold over the league from 1969 thru 2007, taking turns winning the regular season title and earning an NCAA tournament bid each year. The only exception to the dominance that came from Penn and Princeton was Brown University. The Bears won the title once during that period, in 1986.

The landscape of the Ivy League, however, experienced a seismic shift in the fall of 2007. Cornell displaced perennial powerhouses Penn and Princeton by winning back-to-back Ivy League championships in the 2007-08 and 2008-09 seasons. In doing so, they became the first team in school history to earn consecutive trips to the Big Dance, the NCAA Division I collegiate basketball tournament.

A team comprised of talented and experienced upperclassmen, The Big Red entered the 2009-10 season intently focused on winning a third straight Ivy League title. More importantly, they wanted to prove they could not only survive, but thrive, in the Madness of March.

Consecutive losses to Stanford and Missouri in the NCAA tournament the prior two seasons were extraordinarily motivating as the new season approached. It wasn't acceptable to just get to The Dance, it was time to advance.

Cornell's head coach, Steve Donahue, understood the critical importance of mental strength training. He believed his team was poised to do something very special.

"I have a group this year that I know can win," he said. "They have grown up together and matured on and off the court. I don't know if they know how good they can be. I think they do when playing our Ivy League schedule, but we want more this year."

4 Techniques to Access and Master Your Zone

He continued, "I believe we can play with anyone in the country. I want this group to really believe we can win and advance in the tournament."

Donahue, entering his tenth season at Cornell, was interested in a positive psychology workshop that would enable each member of the program to maximize their confidence and ability.

I led the players and coaches through my peak performance training program on Halloween weekend, a couple of weeks before the first official game of the season. The training consisted of teaching about The Toxic Three of Poor Performance and The Big Three of Peak Performance, other principles of positive psychology, and an extended guided zone exercise.

The training was energizing and of value to the entire basketball program. I would soon learn, however, that there was one player in particular who experienced something of a miraculous transformation that would change everything as he knew it.

Who is Jon Jaques?

Jon Jaques was a senior forward for the Cornell Big Red during the 2009-10 season. In his first three seasons Jaques played a total of 108 minutes. He averaged 1.3 points per game as a freshman, 0.9 points per game as a sophomore, and 0.8 points per game as a junior.

Coach Donahue explained that the 6' 7", 220 pound Jaques "was incredibly hard on himself. He's an above average three-point shooter and a tough rebounder and defender in practice."

I learned that Jaques' incessant self-criticism prevented him from consistently playing well in practice but was devastating to his performance in games.

Donahue elaborated, "When Jon misses a shot or has difficulty running drills in practice, he destroys himself. I mean, he gets so upset he becomes a liability. We (the coaching staff) have seen the productive player we know he can be in practice. We just can't trust him in a game. He's such a great kid. He really needs to take it easy on himself."

Jaques, fully aware that he would only play in games that were decidedly one-sided this season, was nonetheless extremely happy to practice hard and enjoy the journey of his senior year. He was so liked and respected by his Big Red family that he was chosen to represent the team as one of the tri-captains for his senior season. He also was excited, for the third consecutive year, to write a weekly article for the New York Times, The Quad blog, chronicling the basketball season to come.

The Quad: The New York Times College Sports Blog
Getting Into the Zone at Cornell
By Jon Jaques, November 12, 2009 9:27 pm

Athletes, whether collegiate or professional, are always looking for unique ways to get an edge. At Cornell, we're no different. Before my sophomore year, we experimented with team yoga sessions (we were led by a free-spirited instructor simply called Hawk) and before last season we received a lecture from James Maas, a renowned sleep expert and Cornell professor. He told us about the importance of getting sufficient sleep for peak athletic performance. While we stopped doing yoga after that preseason and I personally have not changed my erratic sleep habits since that seminar, we have won two Ivy League championships, so those unique experiences could not have hurt. The experimentation continued last weekend, as Coach Donahue brought in Joe Dowling, a peak performance psychologist from Philadelphia who told us that the key to reaching your maximum athletic potential was finding "the zone."

According to Dowling, getting into the zone allows an athlete to focus completely on the task at hand and not worry about anything else but the next shot, play, etc. In most sports, but in basketball especially, it is really easy to be frustrated by a missed shot or a turnover and let that snowball into three or four more bad plays or a bad week. Dowling said practicing relaxation techniques like deep breathing ("in through the nose, out through the mouth") or visualizing playing well in the future can help you focus on the next play or simply drown out negativity in your life and help you sleep better at night.

Anyone who has ever played ball with me knows I am ridiculously hard on myself (more than you would believe). Though I've improved in this area, three and a half years into my college career I honestly still sometimes dwell on bad plays. One message that Dowling left that has really helped me is the idea that "the next shot is the first shot." I'm not at all qualified to be giving psychological advice, but just saying that little quotation to myself on or off the court whenever I feel myself getting frustrated kind of clears my mind and helps me focus. Try it.

After his lecture, Dowling . . . put us in a deep, relaxed state. After what felt like five minutes, we (came back) feeling very relaxed but confused. We found out that each of us had actually been (in a zone) for more than 20 minutes. The last thing I remembered was Dowling telling all of us to try to watch the colors of our inner eye float around while our eyes were closed. Do it . . . really trippy stuff.

Anyway, our first game of the season is finally here: at Alabama on Saturday. As much as my teammates and I love two and a half hours of practice a day for a month straight, it's about time we played a real game . . .

November 14, 2009: The Season Opener
A Bench with a View

Jon Jaques did not play in the 71-67 opening win against Alabama. He remained a DNP (did not play) on the stat sheet for the next two games versus the University of Massachusetts and Seton Hall. Jaques then played one minute in a loss at Syracuse and one minute in a win against Toledo. He was called upon to play two minutes in a home win over Vermont.

The season began on a positive note as Cornell started the year at 4-2 against excellent non-conference competition. Jon Jaques readily settled into his familiar role as supportive teammate and bench dweller.

A World of Infinite Possibilities

It's fair to say that at this juncture in Jon Jaques' college basketball career he had no idea of how the universe would conspire to rock his world. To reiterate: In his first three seasons as a member of the Big Red basketball team, Jaques played in only 34 of Cornell's 87 games. He averaged one point and three minutes in those contests.

November 29, 2009: Game #7:
Cornell versus Drexel
Fall in Philadelphia

Drexel University borders the University of Pennsylvania in the University City section of Philadelphia. As I made the 15 minute drive from my home in Manayunk, I was excited for the chance to see The Big Red battle the Dragons of Drexel University in The Legends Classic tournament.

Having conducted the ZONEfulness® (though I had not yet coined the term) workshop only a month earlier, I had a vested interest in Cornell's success. With tip-off scheduled for 2:30 p.m. on a sunny autumn afternoon, I was utterly unaware of the extraordinary significance this game would prove to have on Jon Jaques' life.

Jaques was inserted into the lineup in the second half of the Drexel game after starting forward, Alex Tyler, suffered a calf injury. He responded by playing 15 minutes of tenacious defense and hitting two clutch foul shots to seal the victory.

Coach Donahue, impressed with the role Jaques played in the win, nominated him as the Cornell representative to the all-tournament team.

"I felt it was the last we'd see of Jon Jaques," Donahue said. "I just thought I would reward him by playing him, for what he's done over the last three years in accepting his role. That was my goal. Little did I know he would end up being one of our best players the rest of the season."

December 6, 2009: Game #9: Cornell versus Saint Joseph's
Open the Flood Gates

In his first ever collegiate start, Jaques played 23 minutes and scored 15 points as the Big Red defeated the Hawks of Saint Joseph's.

Two weeks later, on December 20th, he played 12 minutes and contributed 5 points in a win against Davidson University in the first game of the Holiday Festival at legendary Madison Square Garden in Manhattan.

December 21, 2009: Game #11: Cornell versus Saint John's
The Big Apple

The following evening at The Garden, with the game being televised nationally, Jon Jaques officially arrived.

Jaques led Cornell to a most impressive win over an extremely tough Saint John's team. He did so by playing 26 minutes, shooting 7 for 8 from the floor, 5 for 6 from the 3-point line, and scoring a team high 20 points while playing his trademark intense defense.

Jaques said, "The biggest improvement in my game is my individual confidence. You can be as talented as you want, but if you don't have the confidence to go out there and perform in a game, you're going to struggle.

"Dowling came in and talked to us about the importance of forgetting the last play—whether it was good or bad—and moving on to the next one as a fresh start. That kind of hit home with me. I've always been my biggest critic. That's probably been one of the reasons I've not had a lot of confidence in the past."

March 16, 2010
3-Peating and the Big Dance

Cornell did indeed win their third straight Ivy League Championship by going 13-1 in conference play. They earned their third straight automatic bid to the NCAA tournament and finished the regular season with a 27-4 record.

Jon Jaques started 22 games for the Big Red. He averaged 8 points per contest and shot 50% from the floor while leading the team in taking defensive charges. And guess who led the Ivy League in overall 3-point shooting percentage. That's right. Jaques shot 39 of 80 from behind the arc for the season.

"In my 25 years of coaching, I've never experienced anything like it, and I think the rest of the league feels the same way." Coach Donahue continued, "Yeah, he hadn't played in three years, essentially not a meaningful minute, which is hard to imagine, but the difference he's made is phenomenal. I think he's taken our team to a new level."

And they were just getting started.

March 19, 2010
Jacksonville Veterans Memorial Arena, Jacksonville, Florida
NCAA Tournament, Round 1
#12 Seed Cornell versus #5 Seed Temple

Cornell won their first ever NCAA tournament game and became the first Ivy League team since Princeton in 1998 to advance past the first round. The Big Red rather easily disposed of Temple, winning 78-65.

Senior Louis Dale led Cornell with 21 points and contributed 7 assists while the Big Red shot 56.3% from the field. They hit on 9 of 23 3-pointers and committed only 11 turnovers.

Jon Jaques played 34 minutes and contributed six points and four rebounds.

March 21, 2010
Jacksonville Veterans Memorial Arena, Jacksonville, Florida
NCAA Tournament, Round 2
#12 Seed Cornell versus #4 Seed Wisconsin

Cornell continued its historic run through the heart of March Madness with an unbelievable 18-point win over the 4th seeded Wisconsin Badgers.

Cornell's extraordinary seniors once again broke the game open with an early run and coasted to the finish line. Lois Dale had a career-high 27 points, Ivy League player of the year Ryan Whitman scored 24, 7-foot center Jeff Foote contributed 12, and Jon Jaques chipped in with 9 points.

The win propelled the 12th seeded Big Red into the East Regional semifinals—the Sweet 16. The game was played just an hour from Cornell's Ithaca, New York campus at the Carrier Dome in Syracuse, against the top seeded Kentucky Wildcats.

ZONEfulness®

March 25, 2010
The Carrier Dome, Syracuse, New York
The Sweet 16
#12 Seed Cornell versus #1 Seed Kentucky

Playing on the campus of neighboring Syracuse University, this epic event in the history of Cornell University athletics was essentially a home game.

The Newman Nation (Cornell's fans were nicknamed for the arena namesake where the Big Red plays their home games) were out in force. An endless sea of red engulfed the tiny specs of Kentucky blue throughout the enormous Carrier Dome.

After trailing by 16 at halftime, Cornell was able to cut the lead to 6 late in the game. But that was as close as they would come as the game deteriorated into free-throw practice for the Wildcats. The Cornell dream season came to an end as the Big Red fell to Kentucky 62-45.

As the game rolled to its anticlimactic ending, The Newman Nation began chanting: "Thank you, seniors! Thank you, seniors!"

Coach Donahue said after the game, "I've been in this league for 20 years, and I've had three NBA players on one team (at the University of Pennsylvania) that didn't accomplish nearly what this team accomplished. I know it sounds corny, but they love each other more than any other team in this tournament, in my opinion. That's why we're good."

Cornell finished the season with 29 wins and 5 losses and a historic appearance in the Sweet 16.

Jon Jaques started and played 18 minutes with 0 points in his final college game.

But he still had one final chapter to write.

July 1, 2010
Professional Basketball, Really?

Jon Jaques signed a 1-year contract with Ironi Ashkelon to play professional basketball in Israel's top division for the upcoming 2010-2011 basketball season. He joined teammates Louis Dale and Jeff Foote, who each signed professional contracts overseas.

Dale signed with BG Goettingen, a German team that won the 2010 EuroChallenge Championship. Foote was drafted to play about 40 minutes from Jaques, for the Maccabi Tel-Aviv team in Israel.

Cornell's all-time leading scorer, Ryan Wittman, signed with the Boston Celtics as a free agent and played in the NBA's Orlando summer league.

July 9, 2010
A Wild Ending

Jon Jaques said, "It's wild. I think part of the reason I was (initially) resistant to playing was that until two, three months ago, I never thought of myself as a pro basketball player. Now, it's kind of unbelievable being paid to play basketball, basically have a job playing basketball. So many people would kill for it; it's pretty remarkable."

Jon Jaques embraced the most critically important component of The Big Three of Peak Performance: Extreme Self-Support! As the next shot became the first shot, every day became an opportunity for him to support himself. This enabled him to connect with his zone, to trust himself at an incredibly high level, and to achieve beyond his wildest dreams.

Coach Donahue had one final tribute for Jaques: "He's gone from a kid who I would worry about his poise, to . . . if there was a more poised player on our team, I don't know who it is.

I'll use him as an example for kids for as long as I'm coaching—never give up!"

Epilogue
March 24, 2011
Ashkelon, Israel

Jon Jaques continued blogging as he began his professional basketball career in Israel.

The following excerpt comes from an article he wrote for SI.com as his first year as a pro hoopster came to a close.

Unless things change in a hurry, I could be flying home sooner rather than later. Ashkelon is 5-17 on the season, sitting in ninth place, and three games out of the final playoff spot with five games to go. So, yeah . . . a year removed from being near the top of college basketball I am at the bottom of Israeli basketball.

As a first year pro that wasn't planning on a career in basketball three months before this all started, I couldn't be prouder of my individual performance and effort this season. The numbers aren't great or even decent (I'm averaging only 3 points, 3 boards in about 12 minutes a game), but this season was way more about personal growth than stats for me anyway. Plus, I can always tell my grandchildren someday that I led the Israeli Premier league in fouls per minute (like a wise man once said, "If you're not fouling, you're not playing defense"). There's a chance I will retire from pro basketball after one season, though I have not decided anything officially yet. My ultimate goal for the future, whenever I do decide to call it quits, is to have a successful career writing about the sport. If I can write a college basketball blog while playing overseas, I'm excited to see what I can do when I'm living in the same hemisphere as the games I'm covering.

Jaques did retire after one memorable year playing professionally in Israel.

He spent the 2011-12 and the 2012-13 seasons coaching in the Ivy League as an assistant coach at Columbia University.

For the 2013-14 season, Jaques returned home to Cornell to begin his tenure as an assistant coach for his beloved Big Red.

He continues to write . . .

Opening Rant About Self-Criticism

When I prepare to facilitate a ZONEfulness® workshop for a team or present my "How to Become Smart Enough to Know When to Stop Thinking" course at a psychology conference, I always write at the top of my outline, "Opening Rant About Self-Criticism . . ."

After introducing myself to a Division III men's baseball team, I began the workshop by asking the players the following question: "Does anyone beat themselves up after a strikeout or any failure on the field?"

All thirty hands went up.

"How does that work for you?"

Laughter ensued as players begin to contemplate the insanity of self-criticism. And now the rant begins.

"I like to go off about the unbelievably destructive nature of self-criticism. I have tremendous energy about the subject. But when I was younger . . .

If medals were given out for beating yourself down I would have stood atop the podium with the gold medal swinging around my neck.

Sure, I was a good point guard in high school and played Division III college basketball, but I was a prisoner of negative, self-critical thinking. I played well in stretches but sabotaged myself all the time.

Self-criticism will keep you from consistently playing well. It is a zone buster. There is no debate about it.

Feel free to get mad about the play, the at-bat, the throw, the slide. But, under no circumstances should you ever take it out on yourself and into the next play.

It's not possible to get into your zone and stay there if you are stuck in the error or the strike out. It won't happen! Trust me on this one. It's not possible to reach your potential if you are wasting your energy on doubting and criticizing your own play.

Now, I'm going to show you how to turn self-doubt into Extreme Self-Support, and how to consistently experience your peak performance zone.

So, who here treats themselves the same way they treat a teammate who, despite playing really hard, had a three strikeout, two error game? Do you talk to your teammate the same way you talk to yourself when you have a bad game?

It's crazy, isn't it? We are incredible at supporting others and getting them back on track. We build them up and remind them how valuable they are to the team. We really care. We want to help!

We slam ourselves but at the same time we go to great lengths to support the people we care about."

And that's when the team ZONEfulness® workshop gets off and running.

Positive Psychology

Self-support is the foundation of positive psychology. It is the cornerstone of happiness and emotional well-being. Whether excelling in your sport or winning the game of life, it all begins and ends with self-compassion.

It's been shown that consistently self-critical people have decreased energy, increased mood swings, and great difficulty enjoying life. Self-criticism is, unquestionably, the most damaging of The Toxic Three of Poor Performance.

Solution-Oriented Questions: Extreme Self-Support

I have asked the following questions of student-athletes to assist them in understanding the extraordinary value of Extreme Self-Support:

- "Who in your family has been extremely supportive of you from the time you first began playing soccer?"

- "What coaches have been emotionally supportive and influential in your softball career?"

- "What specific memory do you have of a teammate being there for you and supporting you after a poor performance on the court?"

- "How do you treat a teammate after she makes an error? Tell me about a specific example?"

- "How does it feel when teammates, coaches, and fans cheer you on?"

- "Can you remember a time or times when you were Extremely Self-Supportive after missing multiple foul shots?"

- "Tell me how you can so easily beat yourself up but so readily support teammates when they have an off game? Interesting, isn't it?"

4 Techniques to Access and Master Your Zone

Strategic Assignments: Extreme Self-Support

- The following homework assignments were given to student-athletes to help them generate, maintain, and appreciate Extreme Self-Support:

- "I know your lacrosse coach has a rough way about him. I know that he is very quick to criticize you and rarely acknowledges your performance and your effort. Before bed tonight, I want you to imagine that you are the head coach. How would you communicate with the team? What would you say to validate and support a player like you? Remember to close your eyes and take really slow, deep breaths. Experience yourself as the coach for 3 to 5 minutes."

- "Before field hockey practice tomorrow do a one minute power zone and promise to be unbelievably positive to yourself and your teammates. Remember, if you criticize yourself, use it as a reminder to support yourself like you do everyone else on the team."

This specific assignment generated a terrific response of Extreme Self-Support:

- "I know you have a long bus ride Saturday morning for the 7 p.m. starting time at the University of Scranton. After listening to your ten minute zone, turn off the recording and imagine—with your eyes still closed—that you are watching a movie.

The lead actor in the movie is a college soccer player who has shifted from being outrageously self-critical his freshman and sophomore years to incredibly self-supportive his junior year.

Watch the movie on the inside of your eyes. Observe his transformation as he lets go of his mistakes and allows every play to be the first play. Visualize and experience his great junior season.

Finally, have fun and be the lead actor in your own movie."

- "Before your training run today, take one minute and review your personal history of self-doubt and criticism. Then, take at least two minutes and do the opposite. Imagine yourself being overwhelmingly self-supportive.

- When you begin your run, remain positive and exaggerate being self-supportive. Have fun. Take it to the limit. See how rapidly you can develop a mastery of Extreme Self-Support."

The Toxic Three versus The Big Three
Round 2: Self-Criticizing versus Extreme Self-Support

Having read this far, I am quite confident that you are fully aware of my position on self-criticism and self-doubt. But I will reiterate once more that the most damaging and debilitating of The Toxic Three is the ultimate zone blocker, self-criticism.

The Poisonous Gas of Self-Criticism:
Comparing Yourself to Opponents

A most insidious yet subtle form of self-criticism is worrying about the performance of opponents. Many student-athletes have the tendency to obsess on the ability of their competition. Often, they greatly exaggerate the talent of the opposition.

This external focus will dismantle a student-athlete's ability to access the performance zone. It relinquishes all of her personal power when overly concerned about the competition. This form of self-criticism is disrespectful to one's ability, preparation, and zone because the attention is directed externally (at the opposition).

Student-athletes who engage in this anxiety and worry about their competition are unaware that they are preventing themselves from accessing their zone and playing at a high level.

Using Self-Criticism to Your Advantage

"Thank you, self-criticism, for reminding me to be Extremely Self-Supportive." This mantra dissolves the self-criticism symptom and triggers the peak performance zone.

This chapter has ardently suggested that self-criticism is the leader of The Toxic Three of Poor Performance. So, feel free to use self-criticism as an intensely powerful reminder to be outrageously self- supportive. You already know how to support your teammates. Now is the time to do it for yourself!

And while you're at it, use the opposition to your advantage. Whenever you are overthinking or worrying about your individual opponent—or the other team—use it as a positive trigger to believe in yourself.

You absolutely can become Extremely Self-Supportive and completely focused on yourself and your team. This shift will become automatic as you practice using self-criticism to your advantage.

4 Techniques to Access and Master Your Zone

The Honor System

The following is an example of an Extreme Self-Support zone exercise I routinely facilitate for self-critical student-athletes:

"I understand that you have developed a pattern of criticizing yourself and obsessively focusing on the mistakes you make during competition. Now, I want you to close your eyes and begin to take five very slow, very deep breaths. Be sure to breathe in through your nose and out through your mouth.

As you focus on your breathing, imagine a teammate of yours who is a good friend. Take a moment and imagine this person being incredibly self-critical after playing poorly.

For the next one minute I want you to continue to explore the intense self-criticizing that your teammate is experiencing.

Finally, I want to invoke the honor system. I want you to be completely honest. For the next one minute imagine what you would say to your friend and teammate. How would you support him? What kind of advice would you give? How would you let him know you really care?

That's right. Be really honest about how you would support him.

I'm extremely confident you can do the same thing for yourself."

Counter-Intuitive

This zone exercise always stimulates an interesting, valuable conversation. Namely, the fascination with the unbridled support we provide to our teammates, friends, and family.

Conversely, with the same ease we berate ourselves, often with great venom, this instinct to emotionally hurt ourselves is the polar opposite of what we do with the people in our lives that we love and care about.

ZONEfulness®: A CASE STUDY
CARL: SELF-CRITICIZING

Our favorite why-ning wide receiver, Carl, was also quite skilled at self-criticizing.

Carl reported that he had continued to play guitar on a consistent basis as our third session began. He felt really positive about shedding his why-ning and focusing on what he could do differently.

However, he continued to self-criticize and worry about his ability to start at wide receiver in this, his junior year. Our session took place after a particularly grueling early-August training camp practice that left Carl completely physically and emotionally drained.

It's important to understand that any symptom, specifically any of The Toxic Three of Poor Performance, is exacerbated when you are over-tired. Why-ning, self-criticizing, and what-ifing become magnified when exhausted.

As Carl stressed out about "being the odd man out" of the receiver rotation for the upcoming season he began questioning his ability.

"I will probably be the fifth receiver. Maybe I should have gone Division II instead. I dropped two balls today. Maybe I don't belong at this level."

Now, I already knew that Carl was a fast, highly-regarded receiver in this program. He had even started five games his sophomore year when the team's best wide-out was injured.

I also understood that Carl was a great cheerleader. He loved to help his teammates when they were down. Carl was all about the team "as family."

So, I declared that the honor system would be required of Carl for him to fully benefit from our work for the remainder of the session.

After agreeing to be 100% honest I told Carl to close his eyes and focus on very deep, slow breaths. As he imagined his closest friend on the team beating himself up after playing poorly, I requested that he keep his eyes closed and tell me how he would support his friend.

Carl began, "Well, I would tell him to keep his head in the game."

"Talk to him as if he were here, " I said.

"Stay in the game, dude. We need you, Anthony. We're in this together. Stay tough. I know you can dominate him. Let's go."

Carl and I processed the counter-intuitive nature of brutally criticizing one's self while seamlessly supporting teammates for the next few minutes.

I then ended the session with a trademark rant about self-criticism being the most powerful and toxic of zone blockers. Carl seemed relieved as he smiled at my consistent stance on the poisonous nature of self-criticism.

Carl's homework was to be Extremely Self-Supportive. Specifically, I told him to be "unbelievably nice to yourself just like you are with teammates."

With the opening game just a few weeks away, Carl was receiving the principles of ZONEfulness® with an openness that would enable him to create consistent peak performance.

Support from Family, Friends, Coaches, and Teammates

"My mom called and said, 'you almost had that one.' Moms are the greatest. You can't do wrong by mom. She blames it on everyone else but me." — Joel Dreesen, Former New York Jets 3rd String Rookie Tight End, after dropping a pass.

Solution-oriented questions and strategic homework assignments frequently involve experiencing your history of emotional support from others as well as imagining how you would want a teammate to support and care for herself.

We can't do it alone. Extreme Self-Support is something that is born out of our interaction with the valued people in our life. Specifically, our family, friends, coaches and teammates want us to be self-respectful and self-supportive.

I routinely ask the self-critical, self-doubting student-athlete the following questions:
- "Why do you have one set of rules for yourself and another set for everyone else?"

- "Would you ever advise a teammate to severely criticize herself the way you talk to yourself?"

I've grown accustomed to the looks of confusion I receive from these clients.

They communicate to me with their looks that I must be crazy. Verbally, I typically receive something like this: "I would never talk to a friend the way I talk to myself. Why would I do that? I'm not brutal like that."

It almost makes me feel like I should be the one giving a confused look. So, we talk about it. I invoke the honor system. I work to get a buy-in and a commitment to having one set of rules:

Rule #1—Focus on being a positive, emotional support to yourself the same way you are to your teammates.

Rule #2—Remember to be honest. Ask yourself, "Would I ever verbally attack a teammate the way I do myself?"

Rule #3— Review the experiences you have had with supportive family members, friends, coaches, and teammates. Perhaps there is one person in particular who has been extraordinarily supportive. How does this person want you to respect and support yourself?

The family is a team. The team is a family. We are all connected. We all want our loved ones to be happy and content. Learn from your history of being supported. Imagine how you will treat your future friends and teammates, the players you coach someday, the kids you parent.

Feel the freedom to shred the self-critical, self-doubting set of rules.

Be psychotically self-supportive! It's a lot of fun.

5th Sport Psychology Session with Owen, Late March, 2013

Owen entered my office on a cold, windy late-March evening. Having recently returned from Florida he was sporting a healthy tan after having played five games in the Ft. Pierce sunshine.

As Owen began to speak he broke into laughter. "It was unbelievable! I was actually really good. I couldn't get over how confident I was at the plate. I hit the ball really hard. I had five singles and two doubles. I even got robbed a couple times on some line drives. I could have easily had more."

I asked Owen how this year was different from his sophomore year.

"Well, I was just really anxious back then. I wasn't there mentally. Now, I don't know, I just feels good. I'm really comfortable at the plate. I know how to focus on every pitch. You know, every pitch is the first pitch. And I don't beat myself up or do the what-if thing anymore.

Oh yeah, I have to tell you what happened when we played UMASS (University of Massachusetts).

This is great. I was batting with a man on second. I saw that he was trying to steal third so I stepped back. When the catcher threw the ball it hit me in the back of the helmet. Then he started yelling that I interfered and pushed me hard in the back.

Before, I would have probably been intimidated, especially because he's a college kid. But I got pissed off and yelled back at him. The umpire separated us and told us to calm down.

Here's the best part: I stepped back into the batter's box and I was even more in my zone! I was fired up. "

"So what happened?"

"I ripped an RBI single!"

I communicated to Owen that he was excelling in his mental-strength training. He was building his Personal History of Success file while becoming Extremely Self-Supportive.

I knew this because he was so upbeat and happy. When people embrace The Big Three of Peak Performance they feel great. When immersed in The Toxic Three of Poor Performance they feel awful.

We discussed in detail this deceptively simple philosophy of magnifying the good and embracing Extreme Self-Support.

Toward the end of the session Owen wanted to know if we had time to do a zone exercise. As he focused on five slow, deep breaths in through the nose and out through the mouth, he kept his eyes open. After a few minutes he closed his eyes and fully immersed himself in the peaceful confidence of Extreme Self-Support.

We completed the zone exercise and Owen requested that we meet before the official start of the season in mid-April. After scheduling the appointment I told him to come prepared to explore his Future Memories of Success zone.

Extreme Self-Support and the Power of Now

"Forget past mistakes, forget failures, forget everything except what you do now, and do it." — Unknown Lacrosse Player

Personal History of Success, of course, involves transporting yourself back in time to reconnect with your best past experiences in your sport.

Future Memories of Success (which will be discussed in chapter 7) is precisely what its name suggests: Transporting yourself forward in time to connect with your best future experiences in your sport.

These two components of The Big Three of Peak Performance are immensely effective mental strength-training techniques.

Extreme Self-Support is about embracing the power of now. Student-athletes who stay in the moment, for example, by intently focusing on each play, pitch, shot, save, pass, etc., are respecting themselves, their team, and their sport.

The power of now allows for real-time optimal play and performance. When the lights go on and it's time to compete, in practice and in game competition, absorption in the now is a critical component of success.

4 Techniques to Access and Master Your Zone

This capacity to be in the moment is a foundational aspect of self-support and peak performance. It creates and accelerates self-confidence and self-trust. It focuses attention internally and enhances the zone.

So practice the power of now. Feel free to magnify your intensity in practice; create powerful zone states in games; intently focus on each play, drill, set, and sprint.

Remember, you play like you practice.

Being Perfectly Imperfect: The Gift of Failure

"I've missed more than 9,000 shots in my career. I've lost more than 300 games. 26 times, I've been trusted to take the game winning shot and missed. I've failed over and over and over again in my life. And that is why I succeed."
— Michael Jordan, Extremely Self-Supportive,
Iconic Basketball Player.

ZONEfulness®: A CASE STUDY
"I ALWAYS FOCUS ON FAILURE!"

A collegiate soccer player sought ZONEfulness® training in the summer of 2014.

Mara was entering her senior year at a Division III college. Having "played average" as a sophomore and a junior, she wanted to "really have an impact and make a difference" in her final season.

She elaborated, "The main reason I'm here is because I'm freaking out over the strength and conditioning test coming up next week. It took me three attempts to pass last year and, well, if I don't pass, I know I'm going to be on the bench. I just know I can't do it. I always focus on failure. I think I try to be perfect and then I can't do anything. I don't know what's wrong with me!"

Mara explained that she had come across my website and wanted to attend a session because she was desperate to pass the test. Mara also admitted that she wasn't sleeping well and was obsessing "around the clock" that failure was inevitable.

I learned that Mara had always been an excellent student. She excelled as a three-sport athlete in high school but had chosen to focus on soccer in college. Her Personal History of Success, though most impressive, had been devalued due to extreme self-doubt and intense self-criticism.

She listened to me talk about ZONEfulness®; the conscious mind versus the subconscious mind; The Toxic Three versus The Big Three; and about another college soccer player I had worked with earlier in the summer. But Mara seemed distracted and doubtful.

"Do you think this sounds too good to be true?" I asked in response to her non-verbal communication. As Mara shrugged her shoulders, I continued. "Sometimes I get tired of hearing myself talk. Let's show you how to go into a comfort zone." Her doubt shifted to curiosity. "O.k., I guess I'll give it a try," she said.

The session began with an extended warmup of deep breathing. Mara was now ready to experience her comfort zone. Throughout the 15-minute zone exercise I shared stories about three student-athletes.

4 Techniques to Access and Master Your Zone

The three student-athletes I talked about, though of different ages and sports, had a common bond. They had shifted out of the toxic gas of self-criticism and doubt, and into the rarified air and freedom of Extreme Self-Support. I detailed how each student-athlete had used self-criticism to their advantage; how they were able to creatively get out of their own way; and how they were now impactful team leaders who made a huge difference by role modeling Extreme Self-Support.

Mara was in desperate need of a mental break. Her symptoms, her zone blockers, were depleting her emotionally and physically. As she sat incredibly still throughout the zone, she absorbed herself not only into the cushions of the couch but into the experience. I noticed how her facial muscles relaxed as her breathing became slow and rhythmic. I was certain she was accessing the regenerative energy that lives in her subconscious.

Upon completing her zone exercise, Mara opened her eyes and quietly said, "That was awesome. How long was that?" She was pleasantly surprised at the length of time while just as curious about how comfortable her body felt.

After discussing the critical importance of self-support for the remainder of the session, I gave Mara her homework assignments:

1. With the strength and conditioning test seven days away I know you will be ramping up your training and preparation. So, before your daily workouts do a three minute power zone and imagine yourself as a role model for your teammates who specializes in Extreme Self-Support.

2. Make at least three perfectly good mistakes and allow yourself to be perfectly imperfect. Trust yourself to know what this means and we'll discuss next session.

3. Congratulate yourself on setting out to become an expert at Extreme Self-Support.

Mara arrived for her second session the day after easily passing her conditioning test. Her smile told me everything I needed to know but I thoroughly enjoyed listening to her describe her achievement.

"It was so weird because I don't remember exactly everything you said about the girl from the zone thing we did. But I had a strong feeling that I really should take care of myself in the same way. I mean, why not support myself the way I always do with my teammates? It's crazy to pressure myself. I can't believe I've done that my whole life.

Anyway, I did the power zone before my workouts. I saw myself as a team leader, the person the underclassmen looked up to. I imagined myself making a difference. I even imagined myself scoring goals!

And I think I know what perfectly imperfect means. It's the same thing as being really self-supportive. Basically, no one is perfect and if you try to be you will fail. So, just do the best you can. That's what I think it means."

With vigor and energy, she continued, "I did make mistakes, or maybe I should say I didn't do perfectly during my workouts. But it was o.k. I actually did really well getting ready for the test. And the day of the test I was pretty calm. It was kinda funny because I just had this feeling that it was all going to work out. And it did!"

Blue Clips and Visual Imprints

"I like the challenge of getting players to rise to certain levels, but that's the easy part. The biggest challenge is to get them to believe in what we're doing. They have to understand that it's o.k. to have good days and bad days."
— Dawn Staley, retired WNBA all-star player and current coach of the University of South Carolina, the 2017 NCAA women's college basketball national champions

Steve Donahue went on to become the head coach of the Boston College men's basketball team after leading Cornell to the Sweet 16. He understood the monumental value of positive reinforcement. This was evidenced in the team video sessions he conducted with his players the day after games.

These video sessions always began with Blue Clips, which essentially are highlights of what each player did well in the game. Whether it was the star of the team who scored 25 points or a reserve player who worked hard on defense during his five minutes of playing time, the Blue Clips created tremendous validation and support for each member of the team.

Players were given the opportunity to cheer for each other during the film sessions. They also felt the positive energy from the enthusiasm of the coaching staff supporting each individual's effort and performance.

Blue clips are visual imprints of peak performance. This visual evidence enabled players to not only see their performance but to feel the confidence connected with optimal play on the court. It also served as a springboard toward Extreme Self-Support.

In memory studies, it is widely known that people do not forget what they see. Regardless of intelligence level, human beings are much more likely to remember what they visually experience.

With auditory learning, intelligence is a key component to absorbing and retaining information. In other words, intelligence level determines how much information people retain when being taught verbally.

So the Blue Clips that Coach Donahue shows the day after each game not only serve to build support within the team but to simultaneously position each student-athlete to enhance his own sense of self-support and confidence.

The Ultimate Form of Control: Learn and Let Go

"Never give up! Failure and rejection are only the first steps to succeeding." — Jim Valvano, Head Basketball Coach and NCAA National Champion with the North Carolina Wolfpack

I once asked a self-critical college softball player, who was equally motivated and personable, if she thought she would ever achieve her goal of time travel.

"What do you mean?" Abby asked with a quizzical smile.

Smiling back I replied, "Well, you seem really interested discussing, in great detail, all that has gone wrong this season. Everything from going 0 for 5 yesterday to the two errors you made last week, to the game when your coach sent in a pinch hitter for you."

I continued, "It's like you believe you can hop aboard a time machine and revisit your past poor performance. You know when kids say 'give me a takeover, a do over.' Is that what you want? Are you capable of traveling back in time and taking an at-bat or fielding a groundball over again?"

Unquestionably, one of the most pointless, debilitating behaviors that people engage in is the analysis and repetitive review of the negative past. Hence, the age old adage, "You can't change the past" is profoundly accurate.

Of course, what would we do without mistakes? How would we learn? Learning, in essence, would be rendered impossible if we never failed.

There is so much to learn from failure. First and foremost, you can learn to let go of poor performance. This doesn't mean you go into a state of denial or ignore what went wrong, but it does strongly communicate that you focus on the present and the future.

What is a more effective way of playing your sport or living your life: Stressing out about a mistake that can't be changed or being Extremely Self-Supportive in the moment?

Remember, this doesn't imply that you are always happy and in a good mood when you make a mistake. I strongly recommend you play with a fierce passion and commitment to your sport and your team. You certainly can get angry and frustrated after, for example, a missed penalty kick or a turnover, but you must let go of the mistake and cease and desist from attacking yourself.

One more thing, please contact me if you ever figure out how to travel back in time!

4 Techniques to Access and Master Your Zone

The 3 Ts of Dissolving Self-Criticism

A brief tool that summarizes the shift from self-criticism to Extreme Self-Support involves translation, transportation, and transformation.

- Translate: Self-criticism is used as a positive trigger and translated into a fluent language of Extreme Self-Support.

- Transport: Self-criticism is used as a reminder to transport yourself into your zone.

- Transform: Self-criticism is the catalyst behind your transformation into an Extremely Self-Supportive student-athlete.

A Final Word on GRIT

Angela Duckworth's revolutionary 2016 book, *Grit: The Power of Passion and Perseverance*, is an absolute must read for all student-athletes, as well as their parents and coaches.

Please check out this data driven masterpiece that proves that Grit is a much more reliable (amazingly so!) predictor of success than talent or I.Q. In my work with gritty student-athletes I have found that The Toxic Three of Poor performance, particularly self-criticism, can diminish the benefits of being a hard working, passionate, student-athlete.

I believe that people who score high on Dr. Duckworth's Grit assessment scale can enhance peak performance in their sport, the classroom, and the game of life by becoming Extremely Self-Supportive while using failures and obstacles as opportunities to become stronger and grittier. Find out how gritty you are by going to http://angeladuckworth.com/grit-scale/.

ZONE EXERCISES:
EXTREME SELF-SUPPORT

Guided Zone

You can participate in this zone exercise by going to ZONEfulness.com and clicking on the audio file, **Guided Zone: Extreme Self-Support**.

A reminder: Let yourself fully experience the zone recording by closing your eyes and following the suggestions to embrace Extreme Self-Support.

Self-Zone

When you complete the guided zone recording, remember to practice doing a self-zone. You can go into your self-zone right away or wait a little while, it's up to you.

Begin your self-zone by closing your eyes and taking five very slow, very deep breaths (remembering to breathe in through your nose and out through your mouth).

A self-zone is ideally three or more minutes. Feel free to practice keeping your eyes open for some or all of both the guided and self-zones.

Power Zone

Begin practicing your Extreme Self-Support power zone. This 1 to 3 minute power zone can be practiced almost anywhere and will dramatically help you to experience peak performance while practicing, training, and competing in games. Simply take five slow, deep breaths, breathing in through your nose and out through your mouth.

It's nice to alternate opening and closing your eyes while doing your power zones. Find out what works best for you.

Anchor Zones

Continue to practice your anchor zones on a daily basis. Simply remind yourself to be self-supportive and absorb yourself into the present moment, the power of now, when practicing, training and competing in your sport. See page 33 for more examples of anchors.

Personal Highlight Film Zone

Keep watching the videos of your best performances. When watching, enjoy reconnecting with the feelings of confidence and self-support you are experiencing. You can allow your growing sense of self-assurance and your understanding of the value of Extreme Self-Support to propel you into Future Memories of Success.

Just turn the page.

4 Techniques to Access and Master Your Zone

CHAPTER SEVEN
HOW TO DISMANTLE AN ATOMIC WHAT-IF

TECHNIQUE #3: FUTURE MEMORIES OF SUCCESS

"You can't put a limit on anything. The more you dream, the farther you get."
— Michael Phelps, American swimmer, all-time leader in Olympic medals with 22, including 18 gold medals

ZONEfulness®: A CASE STUDY ON-DECK VISIONS

I have enthusiastically communicated to clients, whether on the high school, college, or professional levels, that mental strength training will serve to separate them from competitors of similar abilities. In other words, skill level is, frequently, remarkably equal between players at any level of competition. The athlete who practices ZONEfulness® will have a distinct advantage over opponents with comparable talent.

Of course, even elite athletes have to deal with fearsome opponents. A client of mine encountered this reality, namely that other players were as good, or as he was finding out, even better than he was, as he embarked upon his professional baseball career.

Who is Mike Costanzo?

Mike Costanzo was always the best player on his baseball teams.

Growing up in suburban Philadelphia, Mike was far and away the most dominant player on his little league and grade school baseball teams. He didn't miss a beat when he entered Archbishop John Carrol High School, starting as an infielder his freshman season. That year the Patriots were the 1998 Philadelphia Catholic League champions.

A power-hitting first and third baseman, Mike was also a great pitcher. As a high school sophomore, junior, and senior he was named to the first team all-catholic and all-city teams. He was also unanimously selected as the Philadelphia city player of the year in both his junior and senior seasons.

In 2012, Mike was named to the first team for the top players in the history of Philadelphia baseball. He is unquestionably one of the most feared power hitters ever to play in the City of Brotherly Love.

Beach Bound

Mike earned a Division I baseball scholarship to Coastal Carolina University in Myrtle Beach, South Carolina beginning in the fall of 2002. The Extreme Self-Support and confidence that he had developed throughout his life and baseball career was ever-present as his collegiate baseball experience began.

Mike embraced his primary role as the Chanticleer's designated hitter his freshman year. Playing a bit of third base Mike didn't disappoint at the plate. He batted .318 for the season while hitting 8 home runs and contributing 36 runs batted in (RBI). He was subsequently named to the second team freshman all-American team.

Sophomore Explosion

What does a .359 batting average, 21 home runs, and 74 RBI add up to? The answer: Being selected as the Big South player of the year and a first team all-American. Playing third base and some first base, while pitching on occasion, Mike not only dominated at the plate but established himself as a team leader both on and off the field.

Mike told me in our first session (which took place in January of 2011) while exploring his Personal History of Success: "I knew then (sophomore year) that my dream of making the big leagues was actually much more of a reality. I was unbelievably confident but also really grateful to be at Coastal Carolina. It was a great time . . . so much fun."

A Junior Launchpad

Playing in his third, and what would turn out to be his final season at Coastal Carolina, Mike's performance launched him into the rarified air of "potential high major league draft choice."

As a junior, Mike put up the following, other-worldly statistics:
- .388 batting average
- 15 home runs
- 66 RBI
- 8 wins and 1 loss as a pitcher
- 13 saves as a pitcher
- The Big South athlete of the year
- The Big South player of the year
- First team all-American as an infielder and a pitcher

Mike chose to bypass his senior year to become eligible for the 2005 major league baseball draft.

He certainly had a most productive, enjoyable stay at the beach.

ZONEfulness®

Draft Day: June 6th, 2005

Mike Costanzo is a lifelong Phillies fan. Growing up idolizing Mike Schmidt (the Phillies hall of fame third baseman and iconic home run hitter) he fantasized about being a left-handed version of the city's greatest professional baseball player.

"The computer was in the basement," Mike told me as he elaborated on his Personal History of Success. My mom, dad, sister, grandma, cousins, everyone was standing around listening to the draft over the internet.

It was surreal, unreal; just over the top amazing! We were all just waiting and then they announced, 'Continuing with the second round, with the 65th overall pick, the Philadelphia Phillies select Mike Costanzo.'"

I learned that the Phillies called Mike immediately after selecting him and invited him to come down to their offices at the new stadium, Citizens Bank Park. Mike, his mom, dad, sister, and agent thoroughly enjoyed the magical 25 minute drive from the family home in Glen Mills, Pennsylvania to the big leagues.

"That was probably the day that my confidence was at its all-time high. It really was one of the best days of my life."

The Next At-Bat is a Professional At-Bat

Mike began his pro career in the summer of 2005 playing for the Phillies rookie ball affiliate in New York State, the Batavia Muckdogs.

"It took almost three weeks for me to hit my first home run. That had never happened to me before."

Mike elaborated that he had started to doubt and criticize himself for the first time in his career due to the home run drought. After hitting his first home run the potential zone blocker of self-criticism was diminished. "When I hit my first long ball it was like I reconnected with my confidence. It came right back!"

Indeed it did. In a half season with the Muckdogs, Mike had excellent power numbers: 11 home runs and 50 RBI, along with a .270 batting average.

Back to the Beach

After an excellent spring training in 2006, Mike was elevated to the Phillies Single-A affiliate on the gulf coast of Florida, the Clearwater Phillies.

"I felt great in Clearwater. I knew I really belonged. I couldn't wait to move up to the next level."

Mike allowed himself to step fully into his peak performance zone throughout the entirety of the season. After hitting 14 home runs and driving in 81 runs he was named to the Florida state league all-star team.

"I was pretty sure—actually I was fairly certain—that I would be called up to Double-A after making the all-star team. It was awesome when I found out officially that I would be going home to play."

The Reading Railroad: No Place Like Home, Part 1

Reading, Pennsylvania is home to the Phillies Double-A affiliate, the Reading Phillies. Reading is approximately 60 miles west of Springfield, Pennsylvania, Mike's home town.

It is fair to say that Mike Costanzo had a monster season in the summer of 2007. Playing routinely in front of family and friends he enjoyed an extraordinarily confident and productive year. His .270 batting average, 27 home runs, and 86 RBI propelled him to elite status in Double-A ball.

Mike told me in our initial peak performance training session, "Well, I made the all-star team in Reading and felt more locked in than ever. I guess I was completely in my zone. I mean, I was incredibly confident and didn't dwell on mistakes. I was a team leader and tried to buck up my teammates all the time. The whole season was great."

He continued with enthusiasm, "I also loved playing for the Phillies. It is such a great organization. I really appreciated having the opportunity to be there."

Mike was naturally magnifying The Big Three of Peak Performance as a Reading Phillie. He understood and validated his Personal History of Success; he was Extremely Self-Supportive; and he was consistently imagining himself climbing the ladder to the major leagues (Future Memories of Success).

Trading Places: The Business of Baseball

The offseason for a professional baseball player is a time to rest and regenerate, both physically and mentally, from the daily grind of playing almost every day for 6 months straight. Mike was not afforded this opportunity mentally.

"I never expected to be traded from the Phillies. I was completely shocked and really bummed out. But then I was traded again. It was unbelievable."

Mike Costanzo was traded from his beloved Phillies to the Houston Astros on November 7, 2007. A mere 5 weeks later, on December 13, 2007, he was traded from the Astros to the Baltimore Orioles.

Being traded twice in a little more than a month is a lot for any player to absorb. Through the winter of 2008 Mike found himself overly concerned and worrying about what the future had in store. He maintained his workout routine in the off-season and prepared himself physically and mentally for spring training.

"I never doubted my ability that offseason but something felt different. I knew it was a business and that I had to work harder than ever to achieve my goals."

And, of course, that's what he did.

Shifting Tides

Mike played the entire 2008 season for the Baltimore Orioles Triple-A affiliate, the Norfolk Tides. Playing at scenic Harbor Park in Norfolk, Virginia, Mike had a fundamentally sound year. He hit .261 with 11 homers and 63 runs batted in.

"I played well but knew I could do better. I was confident after the season ended and worked hard to be ready for next year. I knew I was getting close."

The Unthinkable

Through the first 82 games of the 2009 campaign, Mike split time between the Triple-A Tides and the Orioles Double-A affiliate, the Bowie Baysox of suburban Baltimore.

For the first time in his career, dating back to little league, Mike was having a below-average year. His batting average was in the low .200s and he had hit only 3 home runs.

"It was a rough year and I started to overthink and beat myself up. Then I got hurt sliding into third base and was out for the year."

Mike suffered a torn meniscus and had season-ending surgery. He resolved to work more intensely than ever before to ensure a return to peak form.

"I remember being more driven to make the big leagues than I've ever been in the past after I got hurt. I knew it would be tough but I was really just getting started. There was a long way to go but I was going to do it."

The Toxic Three Arrive

Mike Costanzo was released by the Baltimore Orioles on April 2, 2010; two months shy of his fifth full season as a professional baseball player and five months before his 27th birthday.

I taught Mike about the Toxic Three of Poor Performance in our first session. As I summarized the now infamous zone blockers known to you as self-criticism; why-ning; and what-ifing he jumped in and said, "Exactly! I was asking why this happened all the time and was definitely doing the what-if thing about my future a lot. The self-criticism was pretty bad as well. I just couldn't believe I got released."

Having experienced minor bouts with The Toxic Three on rare occasions throughout his career Mike was now dealing with significant uncertainly and anxiety about his dream of playing big league ball.

What's a River Shark? No Place Like Home, Part 2

The city of Philadelphia has a most extraordinary skyline. One of the best views available of the skyline is from Campbell's Field in Camden, New Jersey. Camden is on the Jersey side of the Ben Franklin Bridge that connects to Philadelphia.

The Camden River Sharks are in the Atlantic Professional Baseball League. They are not affiliated with major league baseball. Only a few miles and the Delaware River separate Campbell's Field from Citizens Bank Park, the home of the Phillies.

In April of 2010, the Phillies were beginning a season that they hoped would culminate in a third straight World Series appearance. They won the Series in 2008 against the Tampa Bay Rays and lost in 2009 to the New York Yankees.

From the time of his release in April, 2010 Mike Costanzo was once again available to be a Phillies fan full time. This reignited fandom did not last long. In mid-April, he was summoned to play for Camden's River Sharks.

"I played 16 games in Camden and really tore it up. It was pretty wild because the Phillies were playing right over the bridge in front of 45,000 people every night. We actually had better crowds than a lot of minor league teams I had played for over the past five years. I think we averaged about 5,000 fans a night. Not a bad crowd for an Atlantic league team.

The thing is, I just wanted to get back playing for a major league organization. Camden was really good for me now that I look back on my experience there. I got back into the flow and regained any confidence I had lost."

As a River Shark Mike hit .278 with 4 home runs and 10 runs batted in. It was time to swim up river.

A Red Letter Day

Mike was signed by the Cincinnati Reds organization on May 13, 2010, just five weeks after being released by the Orioles. He was assigned to their Double-A affiliate, the Carolina Mudcats.

In 88 games Mike regained his form and his role as a major league prospect. He hit .270 with 11 home runs and 50 RBI for the Mudcats. He was even promoted to the Triple-A Louisville Bats for six games late in the season.

Exploring Peak Performance: January-February 2011

It is common knowledge that we live in a very small world. In early January, 2011 Mike Costanzo Sr. reached out to a close personal friend of his in hopes of finding a peak performance, mental strength training coach for his son, Mike Jr.

Mike Sr. approached me at a benefit golf tournament in late September, 2010 after a discussion with his lifelong friend, Steve Donahue. Yes, the same Coach Donahue who led Cornell to the Sweet 16 nine months earlier. Steve was hosting the golf tournament that Mike Sr. and I were attending. Indeed, a small world.

Mike Sr. and I spoke in detail about my approach prior to our tee times. He described his son's goals for the upcoming season and for his career. He also expressed his concern that Mike Jr. was experiencing some doubt and worrying a bit more than usual this offseason.

4 Techniques to Access and Master Your Zone

A few months later Mike Costanzo sat across from me in my home office. This initial session lasted 90 minutes and consisted essentially of a recounting of Mike's Personal History of Success; a detailed discussion of his present feelings of lingering anxiety and his current tendency to engage in what-iffing about his future; along with an extended eyes closed zone exercise.

Mike was extremely responsive to the 25 minute zone experience. "It was awesome! It felt like five minutes," he said as the session wound down. I explained to him that we would make a zone recording on his smartphone in the second session and that I wanted him to do the following homework prior to our next session:

- Practice the 1 to 3 minute power zone three times a day.

- Imagine himself playing at his peak level this spring while practicing the power zones.

- Be overwhelmingly positive about the possibilities that exist.

- Be outrageously self-supportive about the future.

We scheduled an appointment for two days later. "I really think this can help me," Mike said as he left the office.

An Off-Season of Zone Exercising

Mike attended three more sessions in the winter of 2011. He was motivated and interested in the principles of peak performance. His favorite aspect of mental strength training was experiencing the zone both in and out of the office.

In the two zone recordings that we made the primary focus was imagining the future as if it were now, what I like to call Future Memories of Success. Mike was easily able to integrate his enormously successful Personal History of Success into his zone experiences while magnifying his future memories of excelling in the minors and making the majors.

"I love the zone, especially the recordings," Mike said in his third session. I've been doing the power zone a lot. I can feel the energy of playing at my best."

About halfway through this session the "what-if I don't make it" conversation was laid to rest. "Thank-you what-if, for reminding me what-will it be like when I make it to The Show" was fully embraced as Mike learned to transform the symptom (what-if) into the solution (making the big leagues).

Back to the Cats and the Bats

"I listen to you more than I listen to my wife," Mike joked when we spoke over the phone in May of 2011. "I listen to a zone recording before every game and let my breathing trigger my zone. I actually see the game playing out. I can feel the confidence when I'm practicing my zone. It's a great ritual for me before games."

Mike elaborated, "What's great, and really pretty funny, is that when I'm in the on-deck circle I just imagine hitting the ball hard. I can see the doubles and the bombs (home runs) leaving the yard. I sometimes laugh to myself because I'm so focused on success.

I was always pretty positive but now I'm at a much higher level. I can't wait to get back to the plate after I make an out. I just don't get down on myself. And when I do your 'every pitch is the first pitch' thing it helps me to really lock in."

In the summer of 2011 Mike played in 120 games, 73 in Double-A and 47 in Triple-A. He hit .271 with 8 home runs and 36 runs batted in for the Carolina Mudcats and .216 with 5 home runs and 26 RBI for the Louisville Bats.

Even though he "scuffled" with the Bats, Mike remained "outrageously self-supportive" and confident about achieving his ultimate goal.

Power Booster Sessions: January-February 2012

"I wanted to come in because I feel I'm really close to making it. I mean I know I can do it but I've been having some doubts lately. I ask myself sometimes if I'll ever make the big leagues. I also want to do a couple more zone recordings."

Mike detailed how, while he was struggling in Triple-A the previous summer, he was able to remain positive and continue to believe in himself. I validated this accomplishment by commenting, "It's not possible to be successful all the time, but an athlete's mental approach can be consistently at a very high level. Your ability to be strong mentally, specifically by being self-supportive, is a huge strength of yours."

Mike was certainly demonstrating an elite level of confidence and Extreme Self-Support. This allowed him to have an unwavering expectation of making the majors.

The sessions in January and February of 2012 continued to magnify the technique of Future Memories of Success. Even though Mike believed in his ability, it's human nature to have doubts. At 28, he was concerned that he could be considered past his prime if he didn't break through and make the major league roster in the upcoming season.

Future memories were explored by experiencing the sights, sounds, and feelings of playing at a peak level. Eyes open and eyes closed zone exercises were facilitated for Mike and two more zone recordings were made (one 8 minutes long, the other 12 minutes long).

As he sat in his familiar spot on the sofa across from me during our second session in January of 2012, I guided him to close his eyes and take five very slow, very deep breaths. As he created a rhythm of breathing comfortably I said the following:

"Mike you can trust yourself to really enjoy exploring all that you will experience and achieve this spring training, this season. But first, for about 30 seconds, you can transport yourself back to the on-deck circle, playing as a Cat, as well as a Bat. Feel the power, the focus, and the calm of anticipating success.

Now transport those experiences forward in time, floating forward into Future Memories of Success and flow. That's right. Experiencing yourself in the on-deck circle, zoning in, smiling, knowing, really knowing that you are going to hit the ball hard. See it. Feel it. Be there now."

I continued on, "Allow this experience of stepping into the sensations: the tunnel vison of the ball bursting out of the pitcher's hand; the soundtrack of hitting a home run; the feeling of the summer breeze flowing through you all the time, any time . . . because this future time is your time. Feel it now. All the time."

Mike left this session, as he did each time we met, with a powerfully calm energy and confidence about his future goals. In our final session in February, 2012, I simply said to him as he left the office, "Have fun, this is your time."

A Real-Time Dream Sequence

Mike was assigned back to Double-A ball after spring training camp broke in March of 2012. He was now a member of the Reds new affiliate, the Pensacola Blue Wahoos, because of the sale of the Carolina Mudcats.

Mike lasted two weeks with the Wahoos. Stepping immediately into his peak performance zone, he was certifiably on fire the first 11 games of the season.

His .333 batting average, bolstered by 3 home runs and 13 runs batted in triggered his promotion back to the Triple-A Louisville Bats.

Mike gladly reported to the Bats, now one step closer to achieving his goal. Playing consistently well through the second week of May, Mike settled into the grind of playing games every day. He did so with a resolve that followed him from Pensacola.

Scott Rolen was the starting third baseman for the Cincinnati Reds on opening day in 2012. Ironically, Scott is unquestionably the second best third baseman in Phillies history, behind Mike Costanzo's idol, Mike Schmidt.

When Rolen suffered a shoulder injury in early May, the Reds needed to fill his roster spot when he was placed on the disabled list.

A Louisville Bat to a Pink Bat

Mike Costanzo was called up to the big leagues on May 12, 2012. His first game in uniform with the Cincinnati Reds was on May 13, which happened to fall on Mother's Day.

"I was really pumped because my family was in the stadium. My mom and dad, Melissa (wife) and Ashley (sister) were all there. My son Michael actually got to see my first game in the big leagues. It was unbelievable. The game was scheduled to start at 1 p.m. but it was raining and the first pitch wasn't thrown until after 4 p.m. It was cool to soak it all in during the delay."

With both teams using pink bats to symbolize the fight against breast cancer and honor Mothers everywhere, Mike had the best seat in the house for the first 4 ½ innings of his first major league game, the Reds dugout.

In the bottom of the fifth, with the Reds up to bat and trailing 4-2, they had a runner on third base. Starting pitcher Bronson Arroyo was called back from the on-deck circle for a pinch hitter.

Voice of public address announcer: "Pinch hitting for pitcher Bronson Arroyo, Mike Costanzo."

Mike's view was about to get significantly better. "I knew Jackson was throwing gas so I just wanted to make contact and score Ryan from third."

With Ryan Hanigan taking his lead off of third base, Mike settled into his stance and waited for the first offering from Washington Nationals pitcher Edwin

Jackson. Swinging at the first pitch, Mike made solid contact and hit the 95 mile per hour fastball to deep left field. The sacrifice fly was successful as Hanigan scored easily from third base.

As Joey Votto, The National League's MVP in 2010, capped off his three home run performance with a grand slam in the ninth inning, the Cincinnati Reds defeated the Washington Nationals, 9-6.

Mike Costanzo was officially undefeated as a major leaguer.

Derek Jeter Calls Timeout: Yankee Stadium, May 19, 2012

Ten years after being named to the freshman all-American team as a designated hitter (DH) for Coastal Carolina University, Mike found himself in the Cincinnati Reds starting lineup as their designated hitter.

"I was starting at DH in Yankee Stadium. It was a completely packed house. Really an awesome experience."

Mike struck out his first two plate appearances at the hands of Yankee starter, Ivan Nova. "I just wanted to stay in the game," he told me. "I felt good at the plate and wanted another chance."

With the Reds leading 5-3 in the top of the sixth inning, Mike made the most of his third plate appearance against Nova. With one out and the bases empty he roped a hard line drive to left field for his first major league hit.

"The hit was great for me. I had achieved a lifelong goal. But what was really amazing was standing on first base and watching Derek Jeter call timeout. He knew it was my first big league hit so he called time, turned to our dugout and threw the ball in so I would have it. I'll never forget that."

Mike is also credited with the game-winning RBI in his first career major league start. His sacrifice fly to center field plated the Reds sixth run to make the score 6-3. The Yankees scored single runs in the eighth and ninth innings to make the final score 6-5, making Mike's sac fly the difference maker.

There's nothing like future memories making their way to the present.

The Dream Continues

In October of 2014 I reached out to Mike as I sat down to write this section of the book. In our three conversations he was an invaluable resource as we reviewed the details of his journey on the field and his learnings from our work together in the office.

Mike said, "Joe, the thing is, I had to work really hard at practicing my zone. Once I got into the ritual of listening to the recordings, which I did before every game, that's when the zone became automatic when I was playing.

In the on-deck circle, at the plate, in the field, the zone just clicks on. I was completely focused on the game and being in the moment. I was all focus all the time, nothing else mattered to me. The work we did rewired my approach to playing. I was unbelievably calm and able to stay in my zone.

I know we talked about it before, but it's helped so much off the field. With my wife and son, life's pressures. It's something that I have that I can connect with whenever I need to."

Mike played 17 games with the Reds in May and early-June of 2012. When Scott Rolen was taken off the disabled list and reactivated to the major league roster, Mike was sent back to the Louisville Bats for the remainder of the season.

In the ping pong world of professional baseball Mike was signed by the Washington Nationals as a free agent after the 2012 season. He played 66 games for their Triple-A affiliate, the Syracuse Chiefs, in 2013. He subsequently returned to the Reds organization later in the summer and split his time between Pensacola and Louisville.

The 2014 season afforded Mike the opportunity to play just 43 games for the Triple-A Bats. After injuring his back he was lost for the season. At the time of our conversation he indicated that he felt great and was close to 100% recovered from minor back surgery.

Having turned 31 in September of 2014, Mike's dreams are alive and well both on and off the field. He is happily married and completely enthralled with his 4-year-old son, Michael. He also has a number of entrepreneurial business ventures that occupy his time in the off-season.

"Joe, you know, I'm still going for it. I'll be there for spring training in 2015. I've had a blast. I've given it my all and I'll keep going."

4 Techniques to Access and Master Your Zone

Positive Psychology

"The most important shot in golf is the next shot."
— Ben Hogan Hall of Fame golfer

The world's most common symptom phrase is unquestionably "what-if?" This toxic zone blocker is so prevalent amongst student-athletes that I frequently pronounce: "If I were king of the universe the phrase what-if would be banned from all languages. And furthermore, anyone caught what-ifing about future failures and obstacles will be instantaneously banished to galaxies far, far away."

I typically continue with the following multiple choice question: What is a more realistic, interesting, and effective way of living your life and playing your sport?

A.
Overthinking, worrying, and what-ifing about all
that could go wrong in your athletic, academic, and personal life.
OR
B.
Imagining and creating visions and feelings about all that can
go right while enjoying Future Memories of Success
in your athletic, academic, and personal life.

"B," of course, is the deceptively simple answer. The key is to be someone who lives the "B" life. By imagining all that will go right you are positioning yourself to achieve your goals and maximize your performance in your sport and in the game of life.

What-ifing is a proud, long-standing member of The Toxic Three. Using the what-if to your advantage, as a positive trigger, is a sure-fire way to propel yourself into The Big Three, specifically Future Memories of Success.

This now familiar formula involves taking the what-if and transforming it to a what-will. So, "What-if I fail?" becomes "What-will it be like when I succeed?" What-willing is a powerfully calming, goal inspiring tool of solution-oriented therapy and positive psychology.

What-willing is a critical component, a springboard, to experiencing Future Memories of Success. The best part is that your mind can't tell the difference between real and imagined future experiences. Your brain is enabling you to experience the visions and feelings of peak performance as if they were happening in the present.

Zone exercises will accelerate this ability and train your brain to anticipate achieving goals and to consistently play at your best.

Solution-Oriented Questions: Future Memories of Success

The questions I ask student-athletes are designed to provide an orientation to the positive future that exists. The following are examples:

- "Imagine the lacrosse season is over and you had your best year yet. Look back through the season and review all that you did in practice and in games to play at such a high level. Tell me about how you prepared in practice and competed in the games. What did you achieve individually? What did the team accomplish?"

- "How will it feel when you achieve your goal of shooting 90% from the foul line this year?"

- "What will you do differently to set the defensive tone as the starting middle linebacker this season?"

- "As soccer camp nears what will be new and improved about your mental focus as the returning goalkeeper?"

- "How will it feel when you approach every swim meet as if it were your last? How will your focus change? How much more energy will you have?"

ZONEfulness®: A CASE STUDY
THE MIRACLE QUESTION

The miracle question is perhaps the most effective and interesting of the solution-oriented questions that I am able to pose to student-athletes.

I asked the miracle question to a talented high school track athlete. Jamie ran cross country in the fall as well as the mile and the 2 mile in the spring. He came to me at the start of his junior year because of the extraordinary discrepancy in performance times he was experiencing when training as compared with his times competing in races.

"If I ran even close to the time I run in races as I do in training I would be one of the best runners in the state," Jamie explained. "I'm really relaxed and fast in practice but I tighten up on the course. I think to myself, 'what-if it happens again' . . . I can really feel it in my chest. That's when I know I'm done. I know it's the worrying that gets me. It's going to kill me every race."

I soon learned that Jamie had been what-ifing around the clock. He had developed an obsessive pattern of worrying that he would run poorly. The what-ifing catapulted him into major self-criticism and a fear that he would never prove to himself, his teammates, or the world for that matter, what he was actually capable of achieving in the 5 kilometers of the cross country competition.

I then learned that Jamie had run confidently and successfully in the 1 and 2 mile races during the spring of his sophomore year. He explained, "Yeah, that was different. I knew I could do that. I had a lot of confidence." He was unintentionally showing me the talent and potential he possessed. It was time to help channel that same confidence into cross country.

The session proceeded with my inquiring about certain things, namely, "What's so special about a 5k compared to a 2-miler? What-will it be like when you run faster in competition than during training runs?" Of course, I also told some stories and discussed the subconscious mind, ZONEfulness®, and The Big Three and The Toxic Three of Peak Performance.

It then occurred to me that Jamie had the capacity to burst out of his obsessive pattern of what-ifing by answering and, more importantly, experiencing the miracle question.

I began, "Jamie, I have an idea. Let's take some time to do one my favorite peak performance exercises. It's called 'the miracle question.' I'm going to go through it—it's a long question—and then you can give me your answer. So here we go:

We both know that when the session is over you are going to leave the office, get in your dad's car, drive home, at some point eat dinner, finish the homework you mentioned earlier, do the 1 minute power zone we talked about, get ready for bed, go to bed, and finally fall asleep."

Jamie nodded affirmatively while I was describing what he would be doing after the session.

"Now is the part of the question where it's necessary to put your immediate reality to the side. What I mean is to put the worry, the what-ifs, and the fear away so you can really focus on the question. You can always come back to the symptoms later.

"This is the best part. While you are sleeping tonight a miracle will occur. The miracle has to do with the reasons you came here today. More specifically, the miracle is about the symptoms of anxiety that have been holding you back from running at your best.

So when you wake up tomorrow the miracle will have occurred. The question is: How will you know as you go through the day tomorrow that the miracle has actually taken place? How will you be feeling differently? How will you be thinking differently? What will you be doing differently?"

Jamie looked at me quizzically as I continued, "Just have a little fun with this. Imagine that when you wake up you feel energized and motivated. So take it from there. How will you be feeling throughout the day; later in the afternoon at practice; tomorrow night? What will you be doing differently to feel so good? How will your thinking have changed?

Imagine how these changes are in place at next Saturday's race. So what will you be doing differently? How will you be feeling differently?"

Jamie began, "Well if a miracle . . ."

I immediately interrupted, "No, when the miracle . . . "

Jamie responded, "Ok, when the miracle happens I won't be so stressed."

Again I intervened, "Let's flip the 'I won't be stressed' to 'I will be relaxed.' Let's stick with 'I will' throughout your answer."

Jamie continued, "Sounds good. I will be energized when I wake up. I will be relaxed and calm."

"Good. So what will you be doing differently?"

"I'll be confident, I guess."

I enthusiastically bounced out of my chair and announced, "There is no guessing in the miracle. There's no maybe. There's no probably. This is a miracle!"

Jamie laughed and went on, "Got it. I'll be psyched. I'll be pumped for the race on Saturday. I will, like you said, support myself the same way I do my teammates and friends. I will win the race. I will win the state championship!"

"So how will you feel differently?"

"I will be confident. I will be happy because I love to run and I know how well I can run."

I asked, "How will you be thinking differently?"

"I'll be positive. I mean I will be really positive. I will think, wait a minute, I know, I won't think on the trail. I'll just go for it!"

"Wow! What an awesome answer, Jamie. Now THAT's what I'm talking about. Let's finish up with a zone exercise."

The zone exercise consisted of Jamie closing his eyes, breathing deeply, and listening as I reviewed the miracle answer he gave. He fully absorbed himself in the future memories of positive thinking; Extreme Self-Support; and ultimately into the sights, sounds, and feelings of running at his very best.

His homework was to imagine the next day as the miracle day every night before falling asleep. He was then to enjoy living the miracle day every day.

Before leaving the session, Jamie asked, "Why is it called a miracle when I know I can do it?"

"Because it's only a miracle to your symptoms, the zone blockers we discussed. Your best self knows what you can do. And you're right, it's not a miracle, it's who you really are."

Jamie didn't win the state championship, but his team did. Jamie did, however, run extraordinarily well in the final three races of the season and in the state playoffs. He routinely eclipsed his training times in the respective meets while reconnecting with his passion for the sport and event he loves.

Strategic Assignments: Future Memories of Success

I give homework assignments to student-athletes to show them the possibilities that exist. The following are examples:

- Do a one minute power zone three times a day where you experience yourself on the foul line. Mentally rehearse your pre-shot routine. Create a tunnel vision, a visual anchor, on the front of the rim. See, feel and hear the free throw swishing through the net.

- While stretching before the next swim meet imagine yourself surpassing your best time in the 100-meter butterfly.

- I know your favorite player is Mike Trout of the Angels. Later tonight, go to YouTube and watch highlights of Mike's best plays in the field. Then study the video of his focus at the plate as he launches line drives and home runs all over the park. Afterwards, close your eyes and imagine your own future highlight film for this upcoming season.

- Pretend field hockey season is over and you performed at an extraordinarily high level throughout the season. Before bed tonight close your eyes and take five deep breaths. Then really enjoy reviewing all that you achieved from the first game of the season through the conference championship. Magnify the sights, sounds, and feelings of your incredible season.

- "Ask yourself, every day, What-will it be like when I'm the starting midfielder this season. I know you know the answer is, It will be awesome! Ask yourself this question all the time until you are named the starter."

The Toxic Three versus The Big Three
Round 3: What-ifing versus Future Memories of Success
Creating a Positive Self-Fulfilling Prophecy

What-ifing is a guaranteed way to get in your own way. When you say, "What-if I fail?" "What-if I strike out?" "What-if I get cut from the team?" you are greatly enhancing the probability that you will suffer defeat.

What-ifing is a negative self-fulfilling prophecy. It prepares you to fail. The negative energy produced by anticipating failure prevents you from creating your peak performance zone.

What-willing propels you into Future Memories of Success. It positions you to succeed, to play at your best. What-willing is a positive self-fulfilling prophecy. It prepares you to practice your zone and it enables you to enjoy magnifying the future possibilities.

Most importantly, what-willing leads you into your peak performance zone in real time competition. When there's a WILL, there's a way!

ZONEfulness®: A CASE STUDY
WHAT-IF I DON'T GET DRAFTED?

The head coach of a major Division I basketball team asked that I have an individual session with his best player. The request was made on Sunday morning, the day after I had led the team through a peak performance, positive psychology training program. Later that evening the team was scheduled to play their fifth game of the young season.

I readily agreed and met with the player, Jim, at 12:15 that afternoon.

Jim arrived on time and we got right to the business at hand.

"Jim, what would you like to accomplish by coming to talk to me today?"

"Well, I'm just worrying a lot. I know I shouldn't be but I'm really up in my head. The main thing is the scouts. They're here all the time. It's a lot of pressure. What-if I don't play like I did last year? What-if I don't get drafted? I just want to focus and not get so wrapped up in all that stuff."

Jim was still an underclassman but was considered one of the premier players in one of the top conferences in the country. If he played up to his potential this season (his previous year was exceptional) and decided to declare for the NBA draft, he most certainly would have been a selection in the first or second rounds.

I responded, "Tell me about the times in your career when you found yourself what-ifing about what would go wrong?'

"I don't know. I really don't do this kind of thing. That's why I'm worried, because I keep focusing on letting my teammates down; the coaches. It's just really hard."

I knew from my discussions with the head coach prior to the team workshop and right before the individual session that Jim was even a better person than he was a basketball player.

His coach described him as "a natural leader who comes from a great family. Just a great kid who loves life. He's really the kind of genuine kid every coach wants playing for his team."

I felt strongly that Jim could reconnect rapidly with his best self and dismantle the atomic what-ifs that were presently plaguing him. He was a young man who had an impressive Personal History of Success and knew how to support himself emotionally.

The remainder of the session consisted of using what-ifs as a positive trigger to what-will; creating, by what-willing, a positive self-fulfilling prophecy; asking Jim, "What-will it be like when you have a tremendous season?" and "What-will it be like when you have to decide whether to stay in school or enter the draft?"

The toxic energy that accompanied him into the room rapidly shifted into a calm determination.

The last 15 minutes were spent leading Jim into an eyes closed, Future Memories of Success zone. He was extremely responsive and upon opening his eyes stated, "Yeah, I needed that. Thanks. I think I'm good to go."

Jim led his team to a much needed victory about seven hours after our meeting. His 30+ points launched him into another highly successful season. He decided to bypass the NBA draft and remain with his team for the following season.

ZONEfulness®

The Art of What-Willing

What-willing is a powerful technique that certainly will dismantle atomic what-ifs. The following chart can serve as a visual imprint, a reminder, to focus on the Future Memories of Success that are triggered by the creative art of what-willing.

What-Ifing:	What-Willing
What-If I miss a lay-up?	What-will it be like when I drive to the hoop with confidence and finish the shot?
What-if I don't get in the game?	What-will it be like when I prepare myself mentally and only focus on what I can control?
What-if a new recruit beats me out?	What-will it be like when I become an expert at accessing and staying in my zone?
What-if I make an error?	What-will it be like when I let every pitch be the first pitch?
What-if the God's of soccer decide to ban me for life from the sport?	What-will it be like when I imagine myself to be The Ultimate God of Soccer?

What-ifing will keep you stuck. It is not only the world's most debilitating phrase but perpetuates symptoms. It will bounce you back and forth between its friends, why-ning and self-criticism, with great ease as it depletes your energy and spirit.

The answer to the above what-willing questions and, for that matter, to all what-willing questions typically goes something like this:

"It will be great; amazing; awesome; the best; outstanding . . . "

What-willing creates and generates positive emotional and physical energy as it enables Future Memories of Success to materialize in the present.

So what-will it be like when you become a champion what-willer?

4 Techniques to Access and Master Your Zone

6th Sport Psychology Session with Owen, Mid-April, 2013

"If you can BELIEVE it, the mind can ACHIEVE it."
— Ronnie Lott, NFL Hall of Fame Safety

Owen arrived to our session ready to go. He stated, "The weather has been killing us. It's really frustrating. We've had like two games cancelled for cold and a couple more because of rain. I did pretty well in the games we were able to play.

We start league play at the end of the week and I really want to be ready. I think I can do pretty well. But I did want to talk about something. I still worry what-if I go backwards. I mean, I know I'm not supposed to what-if but it still gets me sometimes."

"So you are ready to check out your Future Memories of Success zone," I responded. "But before we do the zone exercise I'd like to hear more about how you felt in the games you played."

"Yeah, I was really focused. I had two doubles in one of the games and a couple more hits in the other games. I played solid at first base. I just want to be sure I do it in conference play."

"So, you have more to add to your Personal History of Success file. You were zoned-in during the non-league games and now you have the opportunity, tonight, to imagine all the success that awaits you as league play approaches."

Owen countered, "You're right, I did really good."

"Now, remember whenever you worry, especially when you what-if, say, 'Thank you what-if for reminding me to what-will. What-will it be like when I zone in, create a tunnel vision at the plate, and imagine myself making hard, solid contact?'"

Owen: "I know I have to do that. I've been doing it but I have to do it more."

"You are doing great. You are absolutely on the verge of trusting yourself at a much higher level. Let's get you ready for conference play."

Owen began the zone exercise in his familiar style of keeping his eyes open and staring at the gold handles across the room. After three minutes he closed his eyes and went deeply into his peak performance zone.

I stated, "Owen, you can take your time and begin to explore the Future Memories of Success that await you for the remainder of the season. Now is just the right time to take your time and launch yourself forward . . . curiously, comfortably, and assertively . . . forward to the night before the fifth league game."

I went on, "That's right, creating an effortless rhythmic way of breathing; experiencing the tunnel vision that intensifies as you stare at the gold handles . . . really finding that inner flow as you experience yourself preparing mentally for the fifth game.

And now, as you close your eyes . . . that's right. You can take a few minutes of real clock time and review the first four games of conference play . . . magnifying the sights and sounds, all the sensations and feelings of playing at your peak level. That's it, revivifying the line drives; the doubles in the gap; the clean picks at first base; anything and everything that happened as you played at your best."

I continued to guide Owen to imagine that the first four games had already been played and he was reviewing, from the perspective of the evening before the fifth game, how extraordinarily productive he was throughout this span of games.

I suggested that he "Take all the time in the world to go through each at-bat and really feel your zone. Experience that intense focus and confidence. Experience the power of trusting yourself at the next level."

As Owen opened his eyes 12 minutes later he said, "I'm glad I recorded that. I'm going to listen to it a few times before the game on Friday. You know, I did see myself getting hits. It was pretty wild. Thanks a lot."

We scheduled our next appointment for early-May, the night before his fifth league game.

4 Techniques to Access and Master Your Zone

7th Sport Psychology Session with Owen, Early-May, 2013
The Lead Actor or Actress in Your Own Movie, Starring Matt Damon

Owen arrived ten minutes early to our session on a perfect spring evening. I was available so I invited him into the office. I could feel his energy as he did a very poor job containing his excitement.

"So how did the games go?"

"Unreal! I had multiple hits in three of the four games. I know I had three doubles and one triple. If I was faster I would of tried to make it an inside-the-park home run. It was great. I was so focused, you know, in the zone.

I have to tell you that I made an error at first base on an easy groundball but I was able to let go of it right away. It was like it never happened. I just got ready for the next pitch and focused on the batter.

Before, I know I would of had a major issue making that error. It would have definitely caused me to beat myself up and I probably would of taken all that negative energy to the plate with me my next at-bat."

Owen smiled as he continued, "The next time I was up I smoked a double down the left field line. It felt awesome!"

"So what's your batting average for the entire season and for just the league games?"

Owen unflinchingly replied, "I don't keep track of my average. I never look at the stats."

"Really?" I responded. "How come you don't keep track?"

"Because it makes me overthink and pressure myself. I know when I'm playing well—and I really am now—I just want to go with it. You know, go with the flow."

I shared with Owen that I thought it was a remarkable and most effective tool to remain zoned-in. I let him know that I had never worked with a baseball or softball player who had incorporated that technique into their mental approach to the game. There is a good chance he will be the one and only.

I continued, "Wow, I love it! You absolutely surpassed your goal for the first four games of conference play. Way to go! Let's keep going. I have something different that we can do tonight."

A favorite positive psychology, solution-oriented technique I employ with student-athletes is called: Be the lead actor or actress in your own movie.

Owen appeared a little surprised when I asked him the following question:

"Tell me Owen, who's your favorite actor? If you had to pick someone to play the part of you in the movie of your life who would it be? Let's narrow that down a bit. Who would play you as the starting first baseman and 3-hole hitter for your high school baseball team?"

Owen replied quickly, "It would have to be Matt Damon."

"What is it about Matt Damon that you like?"

"Well, I've always liked him. Good Will Hunting is probably my favorite movie. I read somewhere that he's a real big sports fan."

"O.k., great. Here we go:

I want you to imagine you are watching a movie about a junior in high school who loves baseball. Matt Damon is the lead actor in this movie. You have just watched the first half of the film where Damon has struggled with self-criticism and what-ifing on the diamond, so much so that it has taken a lot of the joy away from playing the game he loves. You have really enjoyed watching him transform his mental approach to the game, specifically the scenes where he goes to the sport psychologist (laughs all around).

Now, it's time to watch the scenes in the movie that portray the rest of the baseball season. What do you want to see Matt do in each of the remaining league games? How fiercely focused is he at the plate? How is he preparing mentally before games? How self-supportive is he? Really enjoy watching him play at his best, one pitch at a time.

Now, you can focus your attention on the familiar gold handles across from you. That's right. Start watching the movie."

After about 30 seconds Owen closed his eyes. This allowed him to really magnify the experience of watching Matt Damon play him playing ball at his very best.

I continued, "You can stare at the inside of your eyelids . . . experiencing them as the movie screen. Maybe it's 3-D, I don't know. But I do know that you can really enjoy seeing, hearing, and feeling all that Matt is achieving.

4 Techniques to Access and Master Your Zone

Feel the freedom to watch scene after scene; hit after hit; win after win . . . experiencing that timeless sense of moving forward in time with Matt . . . being part of the story. Finding yourself, at just the right time, joining him, merging with him, being zoned in; locked into peak performance.

That's right. You are him. You are the lead actor in your own movie. Feel it. Be it. I'm wondering how much you are going to enjoy watching all the future scenes, the future memories that await you."

Owen opened his eyes and simply said, "That was cool."

His ongoing homework was to listen to his zone recordings, consistently do his one minute power zones, and to keep watching Matt Damon play him at an academy award-winning level.

My Favorite Movie: Hooisers

"Imagination has a great deal to do with winning. I always won in my imagination. I always hit the game winning shot or I hit the free throw. If I missed, there was a lane violation and I was given another shot."
— Mike Krzyzewski, Legendary Hall of Fame
Men's Basketball Coach at Duke University

I frequently talk about my all-time favorite sports movie when working with individual athletes or leading workshops for teams.

Hoosiers is based on a true story about a tiny high school in rural Indiana that won the 1954 state championship in basketball. I highly recommend watching this film. It is not only a great story but it mirrors the energy of this book. Namely, it demonstrates the power of hard work, believing in unlimited possibilities, and trusting in yourself and your team.

Toward the end of the movie Hickory High School somehow finds its way to the state championship game. With a team of only six total players and a student body of approximately 50 students, Hickory was the longest of longshots to make the state playoffs. It's interesting to note that at the time the story takes place there were not divisions in the state playoffs based on school size like today. Hickory was competing against every high school in the state of Indiana, a major hotbed for high school basketball.

ZONEfulness®

Coming from the rural southwest Indiana, Hickory finds itself at the culmination of its dream season: In the state final game against a significantly more talented and experienced team from the big city (at least to them) of South Bend, Indiana. Hickory's players are fearing the worst. I am quite certain that major doubt and what-ifing was coursing through their respective minds.

The scene I love to talk about is when Hickory arrives at the arena the morning of the finals. The team walks into the empty, cavernous arena led by their head coach, Norman Dale. This scene (and the climactic footage of the final game) was actually filmed at Butler University's Hinkle Fieldhouse where the 1954 state championship game was played.

Hickory's players enter the arena with their mouths agape and their eyes darting around the enormous gymnasium. At least 50 times the size of their home court the players appear awestruck by what they are seeing.

At that moment, Coach Dale calls the players to stand under one of the baskets. He instructs the team's tallest player to position himself directly under the rim. He then tells the shortest player, Ollie, to climb up and sit on the shoulders of his teammate.

Coach Dale then hands Ollie a tape measure and tells him to place it at the top front of the rim. He subsequently pulls the tape down to the gym floor and announces, "It's 10 feet."

He then directs Ollie to hop down and stand at the free throw line. Ollie bends down and places the tape measure on the line. Coach Dale pulls the tape to the point on the floor under the rim. He says, "It's 15 feet."

As Coach Dale continues, he points out that he is quite confident that all of the measurements are precisely the same as their home court back at Hickory. As the players let out a collective sigh of relief, they move on to the locker room to prepare for their pregame walkthrough and light workout.

Without explicitly stating it, Coach Dale's communication using the tape measure shifted the team from a potentially paralyzing mindset of "What-if we get blown out?" or "We don't belong in a place like this with an obviously better team," to a position of normalizing that it's just another basketball game on a regulation-sized basketball court.

He was planting a what-willing seed. The message ultimately was, "We've come this far on courts just like this, why not go all the way?"

4 Techniques to Access and Master Your Zone

And indeed they did. In a classic battle that went down to the wire, Jimmy Chitwood, Hickory's star player, hit a buzzer-beater to propel Hickory High School to the 1954 Indiana state basketball championship.

Just as Coach K says, imagination absolutely has a great deal to do with winning. It has even more to do with playing at your best and maintaining peak performance.

A final word: If you are interested in sharpening your imagination and having an enjoyable two hours watching a film about a successful team of student-athletes, do the following: Watch Hoosiers!

Anyone CAN Imagine Anything

"Champions aren't made in gyms. Champions are made from something they have deep inside them–a desire, a dream, a vision." — Muhammad Ali, World Heavyweight Champion boxer

In 1961 Bill Bradley was the best basketball player in the country coming out of high school. He was recruited by national powerhouse programs, but he chose Princeton University due to its reputation for preparing students for high-level government work.

Bradley turned out to be Princeton's greatest player ever. He scored more than 2,500 points while averaging 30.2 points-per-game for his career. Not surprisingly, his name sits atop the majority of Ivy League scoring and shooting records.

He was selected as the NCAA college player of the year in 1965 and won an Olympic gold medal playing for the United States in 1964. Upon graduating from Princeton, Bradley earned a Rhodes scholarship to attend Oxford University in England.

He was drafted by the New York Knicks in 1967 and was a perennial all-star forward over his ten-year career. His Knicks teams won two NBA championships over this time span. He was subsequently elected to the professional basketball Hall of Fame in 1983.

After his professional basketball career ended, Bradley served the nation as a State Senator from New Jersey for 19 years (1979–1997). He unsuccessfully sought the Democratic nomination to represent his party in the 2000 Presidential election.

In his book, VALUES of the Game, he beautifully parallels how the core values of the game of basketball mirror the game of life.

The values he discusses include:
- Passion
- Selflessness
- Perspective
- Leadership
- Resilience
- Discipline
- Respect
- Courage
- Responsibility
- IMAGINATION

An excerpt from his book follows:

Sometimes it's IMAGINATION that motivates you in the first place. It enables you to dream. At one time or another, every kid who picks up a basketball imagines himself or herself a court star.

The basketball hoop in my backyard was erected when I was ten years old. A year later, the wooden poles were replaced by a steel pole and a metal fan-shaped backboard. My parents also laid down a twelve-by-sixteen strip of asphalt and put spotlights on the garage so I could practice after it got dark. I felt like a king, presiding over the Cadillac of backyard courts in our small town. When I was in the fifth and sixth grades, you could find me out there every day after school shooting until dinner. In the winter, I'd wear gloves, a wool hat and two sweatshirts. Occasionally, neighborhood kids would join me in a game of H-O-R-S-E.

I remember the Saturday afternoon in 1958 when the St. Louis Hawks beat the Boston Celtics for the NBA championship. In my mind, I was one of them. I was Bob Pettit shooting the standing jumper, or Cliff Hagan mixing his sweeping hook with reverse layups. Shortly after the game, I went out to the backyard for practice and imagined myself hitting the winning shot. "Four seconds left, three, two—Bradley shoots . . . it's good!"

Nothing unique about that. Thousands of kids all over America, on a winter afternoon at the playground, or out behind the barn, or in the driveway, imagine that they will someday score the winning basket.

It's dropping today . . . all net . . . swish . . . swish . . . just keep practicing . . . just keep shooting.

4 Techniques to Access and Master Your Zone

Imagine your Dreams and Dream of Imagining

"This is the tournament that I always dreamed of winning. This is the first tennis match that I ever saw in my life, when I was 5-years-old. That image stuck in my mind. I'm so grateful for the opportunity and to hold this trophy." — Novak Djokavic, after winning his second Wimbledon Championship in 2014 and his seventh career Grand Slam title

Imagining yourself playing at your best is the essence of the technique we've been discussing, Future Memories of Success. Grade school, high school, college, and professional athletes imagine, while practicing, their dreams coming true on the field; the ice; the court; the track; in the pool; on the balance beam; anywhere they compete.

Perhaps you've had the experience of practicing by yourself and getting lost in your imagination. Was it striking a wicked penalty kick in overtime to win the conference title? Did you break an 80-yard touchdown run on the last play in the Rose Bowl? How about shattering the national record for the javelin throw?

Imagining in this manner trains your brain to anticipate peak performance. So take a minute and remember when you last imagined yourself doing something in your sport that was spectacular. That's right, remember back to when you felt like you were in a dream sequence as you practiced.

Now, start doing it on a regular basis. Enjoy seeing, feeling, and experiencing yourself playing at an extraordinarily high level.

Creating a positive pattern of imagining will frequently lead to dreaming as you sleep. In your dreams you may very well pick up where you left off when you were imagining playing great during the day.

And I know you know that dreams CAN come true.

Just Like Carli Lloyd
July 5, 2015

The United States women's national soccer team defeated Japan 5-2 to win the World Cup, a triumphant performance that was seen by 25.4 million viewers on American television. The size of the audience is a record for any men's or women's soccer game watched in this country.

This extraordinary number of American soccer fans gratefully joined the massive amount of international soccer loyalists to witness one United States player experience her most vivid of dreams materialize on the world's biggest stage.

Just about two months before the championship game, during an intense training session, Carli Lloyd imagined herself having what can only be described as an unimaginable performance in the World Cup finale.

"It's kind of funny, I'm running and I'm doing sprints and it's hard, it's burning, and I completely zoned out. I dreamed of and visualized playing in the World Cup final and visualized scoring four goals.

It sounds pretty funny, but that what it's all about. I think at the end of the day you can be physically strong, you can have all the tools out there, but if your mental state isn't good enough, you can't bring yourself to bigger and better things. And for me, I've just constantly been visualizing, constantly been growing confidence with each and every game. I was on a mission."

Believe it or not, Carli scored three goals in the first 16 minutes of the contest as the American women never looked back on their way to a dominant World Cup victory.

Incredibly, Carli barely missed scoring another goal during her epic opening to the game. Her header, from point blank range, was directed just wide by a couple of feet. Her dream, with clear visions of scoring four goals, came ever so, so close to happening.

Carli Lloyd practices her zone. She takes great pride in mental strength training and has demonstrated her capacity to elicit her peak performance zone anywhere and at any time.

She meditates routinely, takes a ten minute run prior to each match to daydream and visualize playing at her best, possesses great pride in her work ethic, and feels an intense sense of gratitude for her opportunity to play the game she loves.

Carli was awarded the Golden Ball trophy as the Most Valuable Player of the 2015 Women's World Cup. She described her zone beautifully when she said, "I feel like I blacked out in the first 30 minutes or so . . . it's just crazy and unbelievable!"

ZONEfulness®: A CASE STUDY
CARL: FROM WHAT-IF TO WHAT-WILL

Carl scheduled a follow up session in early October, after the fourth game of the season.

Interestingly, he was in good spirits even though he had been given limited playing time. He said, "I think I get it now. The anxiety is just a waste of time. It really brings me down. I haven't come in for a while because I knew I was doing pretty well mentally.

My grades are better than ever and I'm playing the guitar as much as I can. And I do work my butt off in practice. I've gotten in a couple of games and made a few catches but they were after the game was already out of hand. It's all good."

"That's outstanding," I said. "So, tell me, are you what-willing at all?"

"What's that again?"

"It's when you imagine yourself playing and being successful on the field. I usually talk about it in the context of flipping the what-if to a what-will. It's simply taking a 'What-if I don't play the rest of the season?' and saying, 'What-will it be like when I get in and play well?'"

He didn't look certain yet. So I continued.

"It's a component of the technique I like to talk about called Future Memories of Success. It's great you're not what-ifing, but how about imaging your successful future a bit more. There are still six or seven games left this year and your entire senior season.

Let's shift into full-fledged peak performance mode. You have transitioned nicely out of the negativity channel. Let's help you develop a mastery of anticipating success and believing in yourself more than ever."

The session continued with a 20 minute eyes closed, Future Memories of Success zone. Carl recorded the zone exercise on his smartphone. He was, as usual, really pleased with his experience.

Carl never came in for another session. I did speak to him on the phone a handful of times throughout his junior year in college. He remained balanced and acutely aware of his anxiety symptoms when they attempted to attack him.

I was pleased when he told me, "I just use them to my advantage."

Visualization isn't for Everyone

You may have noticed throughout this book that I promote experiencing instead of visualizing. I typically say the following when guiding an athlete during a zone exercise: "And now you really can experience the sights, sounds, and feelings of playing at your best."

I do this because some people are not visual when they are imagining things. Human beings possess five senses. These include:
1. Visual (seeing)
2. Auditory (hearing)
3. Olfactory (smelling)
4. Kinesthetic or Tactile (feeling and touching)
5. Gustatory (tasting)

Each person has a dominant sense or two that they experience when doing a zone exercise. It is, however, commonplace to believe that everyone can visualize. This is not the case. I, for one, can relate to this misunderstanding.

As I learned to do mindfulness meditation and hypnotherapy as a student and a professional I thought I was doing something wrong because I had trouble visualizing whenever I was in my zone. But I could really feel the experience. It was, and continues to be, like a blurry vision with strong feelings pulsating all around me.

So if I were guided to imagine myself staring at point guard for the Dallas Mavericks I would have some trouble seeing myself but, at the same time, I would have incredible feelings of leading the fast break, hitting the three, and passing to Dirk Nowitski for alley-oop dunks.

My dominant sense is kinesthetic, or feeling. As a professional I was able to learn early on that this is normal. But I never know what my client's dominant sense is when we first meet. I keep it simple and give each individual the freedom to follow the sensory modality that best fits them.

So whether someone is visual, auditory, kinesthetic or olfactory (I've never worked with a client who's primary sense was gustatory), allow them to go with their sensory flow. Ultimately, the magnification of your dominant sense or senses leads to feelings of emotional strength and confidence.

So really enjoy seeing, feeling, hearing, smelling, and tasting your Future Memories of Success.

Coach K put it nicely when he said:

"I think you can talk about things and you can see things. But you won't do real well unless you feel it. And we need to put them [his players] in a number of situations prior to that so that when that moment comes, they have already felt that in their hearts. More than anything, more that any offense or defense that I might try to have them do, their being able to feel it is the most important thing for me in coaching my team."

8th Sport Psychology Session with Owen, Late-May, 2013

"Competitive sports are played on a five and a half inch court: The space between your ears."
— Bobby Jones, Hall of Fame golfer

As the session began, Owen candidly stated, "It really is amazing. Basically, I'm playing great. I can't believe how well I'm hitting. We only have two league games left, but it looks like we are out of contention to win the conference championship. I can't believe we don't have playoffs in the Inter-Ac (the name of his conference). But we are in the state playoffs. They start in a couple of weeks."

"So how great are you playing?" I continued, "This is the best part, the fun stuff. We get to talk about your success. Give me some details!"

Owen proceeded to talk about the nine games they had played since the first week of May. He had, indeed, been on a hot streak throughout the entire Inter-Ac schedule. Primarily a line-drive hitter, Owen was accumulating singles and doubles. He had also stroked two triples and two home runs during the conference games.

Unable to resist I asked him, "Have you taken a peek at your batting average yet?"

"No way," he said smiling. "I'll wait until the season is over. I just don't care. I'm just going with the flow."

"I love it. I have to tell you that you may be the only baseball player in the history of the sport who is not obsessed with his batting average. You are absolutely playing at your peak level. Great job!"

Curiously, I asked, "So how was your mental preparation before games? Did you keep up your routine of listening to the zone recordings on the bus travelling to road games and in the locker room before home games?"

"Absolutely," Owen responded. I was doing the power zone in the on-deck circle during games and in practice. I even did them at random times during the day. I think I listened to at least one recording before bed every night this month."

"Well done." I was so impressed. I had to ask: "Hey, something just occurred to me. Do you think you might make the all-conference team? How many teams are there?"

Owen immediately said, "Three."

"I'm feeling first team or definitely second team," I said.

"I don't know about all that," Owen said with a smile on his face.

"We will soon find out," I said with a bigger smile on my face.

Owen requested that we do a zone exercise for the remainder of the session. He felt strongly that the Future Memories of Success technique was a catalyst for his success. "I think seeing and really feeling the future hits and successes helps me a lot," he stated prior to beginning the zone experience.

Owen went, as per his style, very deeply into his zone. Throughout the almost six months he had been coming to peak performance therapy he had, without question, developed a mastery of accessing the zone that lives in his subconscious mind. In my 20 plus years of leading people into meditative zone states, Owen was in the top percentile of clients who have trusted and allowed their subconscious mind to create and generate not only solutions, but optimal performance.

He had demonstrated to himself that the symptoms of anxiety, namely The Toxic Three zone busters discussed throughout this book, were no match for his zone. Owen also embraced the understanding that his best self was infinitely more powerful than any symptom that attempted to steer him off track. He ultimately stepped in to his best self and enjoyed a freedom from worry and a confidence to play at his very best.

This freedom and confidence was certainly present on the baseball diamond but even more noticeable in the game of life.

Many of our discussions that were not detailed in this book had to do with the issues and obstacles that Owen encountered off the field. These issues, extraordinarily normal for any 17-year-old, were still stressful, and at times anxiety-producing. Owen frequently utilized the ZONEfulness® techniques we were processing in our sessions for the real-life problems that he needed to deal with.

At one point he said to me, "Ah, Mr. Dowling, I think I know what's up. What we're doing helps me with everything, not just sports. It's really about being the best person I can be."

9th Sport Psychology Session with Owen, Mid-June, 2013

I have grown accustomed to Owen bringing an enthusiasm with him into our sessions. The energy he exuded on this evening, however, seemed more palpable than usual.

He began, "Well, the season is over. We won two games in the state playoffs. I know that's good but I'm still bummed we didn't win the conference championship. I still can't believe the Inter-Ac doesn't have playoffs. But it was a great year. So I know my average. What do you think it was?"

".350," I said, believing that was a guess on the higher end of the spectrum.

"Try again," Owen said.

".377," I replied with curiosity.

"It was .404 in conference play and .420 for the season. And I made second team all-conference at first base!"

"Awesome!" I said as I sprung up to initiate a high five.

Owen continued, "I just want to thank you for everything. This has really been amazing. I'd like to continue for a few sessions in the summer to get ready for football camp. (Owen was a wide receiver on the football team.) And I definitely want to do some work before and during baseball season next year."

Epilogue

Owen came in for a session in July and for two sessions in August during summer football camp. Now a senior, he was exuding a confidence and an expectation of success for the year to come both on and off the field.

As a junior wide receiver the previous year Owen had 25 receptions and 0 touchdowns. Upon completing his senior season he had accomplished the following:
- Named to first team all-conference as a wide receiver.
- Set the school record for most receptions in a season with 43.
- Set the school record for most touchdown receptions in a season with 8.
- Set the school record for most career receptions with 64.

Owen told me in a session just before Christmas in 2013, "I was the exact same player talent-wise my senior year as I was my junior year. But I knew how to get into my zone and stay there. The worry and the fear I had were basically gone. It's about how I was mentally strong and focused."

Owen once again was selected to the second team all-conference as a first baseman in the spring of his senior year. He hit .370 for the year but stated, "Overall, I think I had a better year this season than last. I hit for more power and felt like I really was a team leader."

Owen was recruited by a number of Division II and III baseball and football teams to play at the collegiate level. There was even a bit of Division I interest in baseball. After much soul searching he decided to follow his dream and attend his father's alma-matter, Drexel University, in Philadelphia.

I have kept in touch with Owen during this fall in Philadelphia as he navigates (with great success so far) his freshman year in college. As a matter of fact he just told me, "I keep using my tools and go into my zone when I study or when I'm taking a test. Oh yeah, I think I might play club baseball for Drexel this season."

ZONE EXERCISES:
FUTURE MEMORIES OF SUCCESS

Guided Zone

You can experience this zone exercise by going to ZONEfulness.com and clicking on the audio file, **Guided Zone: Future Memories of Success.**

A final enthusiastic reminder: Allow yourself to really get into the experience by closing your eyes and breathing slowly and deeply. Enjoy the experience of your future peak performances materializing as you immerse yourself into your zone.

Self-Zone

After completing the guided zone, practice exploring your self-zone. Experience your self-zone for at least three minutes or as long as you want. Once again, the optimal way to create your self-zone is by taking five very slow, deep breaths and alternating keeping your eyes open or closed.

You'll soon discover what style is best for you. Eyes open, eyes closed, or a combination of both.

Power Zone

The Future Memories of Success power zone is 1 to 3 minutes in duration. Step into your future success by experiencing the sights, sounds, and feelings of your goals being achieved.

Pay attention to what sensory modality seems to be most dominant as you explore your future memories. Of course, begin by taking five slow, deep breaths and explore your power zone with your eyes open and/or closed.

Anchor Zone

Build your mastery of peak performance by practicing your Future Memories of Success anchor zone. Absorb yourself into imagining playing at your best in future competitions whether in practice, training, or real-time events.

See page 33 for more examples of anchors.

ZONEfulness®

4 Techniques to Access and Master Your Zone

CHAPTER EIGHT

AFTER STEPPING INTO YOURSELF, STEP-OUT

THE FINAL FOURTH TECHNIQUE: GRATITUDE AND GIVING BACK

"Ask not what your teammates can do for you. Ask what you can do for your teammates."
—Earvin 'Magic' Johnson, NBA Hall of Famer; 5-Time NBA World Champion.

ZONEfulness®: A CASE STUDY
HOW TO GET OUT OF YOUR OWN WAY

A college basketball player left me a voicemail indicating his desire to "get out of my own way so I can play better, uh, what I mean to say is so I can start to play how I know I can play."

As Jim sat across from me during our initial session he launched into a stream of consciousness explanation about his obsession with statistics.

"All I do is worry about my points and rebounds. I feel like I do it all the time, but especially on the court. I do it on the bench when I come out of the game, too. I can't stop. I feel a little crazy, you know, I've never been like this. I called you because I'm starting to think about it all the time off the court. I get lost in it during class, hanging out with friends, with my girlfriend, all the time.

I've been starting since my sophomore year and I love that we are a pretty good team now that I'm a senior. The guys are great and the coaches are awesome. I actually really enjoy helping out the freshman who backs me up. We get along great.

But I'm obsessed with thinking that if I don't average at least ten points a game and pull down six rebounds he'll take my spot. It's crazy. I just can't stop. What's wrong with me? Can you help?"

Throughout our 50-minute session Jim and I talked about ZONEfulness®. After leading him through a 5 minute eyes-closed zone, I sensed that he was still locked in on some nasty self-absorption.

At the same time it was clear that Jim was a thoughtful, caring person. His obsessive thinking had activated the King of The Toxic Three of Poor Performance: Self-Criticism. I knew my job was to continue to do some 'How to Become Smart Enough to Know When to Stop Thinking' therapy when he came back for his second session but I wanted to challenge him with a strategic homework assignment right away.

"Jim, here's the deal. I have a homework assignment that I know will help you. But, I'm concerned that you won't do it with 100% commitment, so I think I'll wait to see if you come back for a second session. I know you're motivated but I'm afraid you may not be fully ready to completely focus on the task I have in mind."

"I'll do anything. You can give it to me now. That's why I came here." I could tell he was eager to jump right in and get started.

Jim passed my "battle for initiative" test with flying colors.

His assignment went like this: "First off, give yourself a well-deserved break from yourself. Here's how: Put the overwhelming vast majority of your energy into giving back to your teammates, coaches, friends, family, girlfriend, strangers, professors . . . anyone and anything that enables you to step out of your own head and take care of others.

In other words, be grateful for what you have and for the amazing people in your life. "

Jim, looking a bit confused, asked what he should do.

"I don't know exactly, just do things differently. I've learned from you that people are becoming exhausted with your statistics obsession. You'll know you're doing the assignment correctly when they look at you the way you looked at me a second ago, you know, a bit confused. When you do things that demonstrate gratitude for the valued people in your life, or anyone for that matter, they'll be pleasantly surprised.

Jim returned five days later for what would turn out to be his second and final session.

"The first thing I did after leaving here was meet my girlfriend at the library. We walked outside and I asked questions about her classes and her friends. I made good eye contact and really listened. She gave me that 'what's going on with you' look the whole time. It was really funny. She couldn't figure it out. I told her about our session and asked her to help me keep going. The rest of the week was just as good!"

Jim went on to detail how he cleaned his apartment (he lived with three other basketball players), did all the wash, and made "a huge pot of spaghetti." He routinely held doors for people on campus; made phone calls to family members he rarely talks to; focused his attention completely in class and asked questions; and "went over the top in practice to focus on playing hard and having fun" while also "being really supportive of my teammates."

We enjoyed the rest of the session talking about the amazingly powerful energy that develops from giving to others off the court and being team driven on the court.

"Thank you, self-criticizing, for reminding me to be GRATEFUL!"

"Many times a day I realize how much my own life is built on the labors of my fellow men and how earnestly I must exert myself in order to give in return as much as I have received."
— Albert Einstein

Team Building

In June of 2015 I was hired to be the peak performance/mental strength trainer for the men's basketball team at the University of Pennsylvania. Penn, a few months earlier, had hired a new head coach, Steve Donahue. Yes, the same Coach Donahue who led Cornell to the sweet 16 and subsequently jumped to the ACC as the head man at Boston College.

"I want you with us from the beginning," Coach Donahue said to me in our initial meeting. "I want this team to grow together and practice gratitude. We need high level communication and, well, I understand fully that we can teach core values."

He went on to elaborate about the five core values that would be the foundation of his new program:
1. Unity
2. Competitiveness
3. Humility
4. Passion
5. Gratitude

As we processed our vision for the upcoming season I felt a powerful wave of gratitude flowing through me. I was being given the opportunity to guide these student-athletes in both individual and team sessions through the entirety of the season.

While talking to Coach Donahue I was able to clearly present a template of ZONEfulness® and peak performance/positive psychology principles designed to magnify play in the game of basketball, and the game of life. Most of these principles have been thoroughly discussed throughout the book and certainly mirror the identified core values.

However, we both knew that a bigger picture was now in play. Ultimately, each member of this program needed to embrace gratitude and learn how to love each other as a highly functioning family in order to achieve the lofty goals that were being put in place.

We agreed that team building meetings would be crucial to transforming the culture of the program and accelerating the understanding that this team was indeed a family.

Coach Donahue ended our discussion by shaking my hand and saying, "Whañau." He explained that he had just completed James Kerr's extraordinary book, Legacy: What the All-Blacks Can Teach us About the Business of Life, which chronicles the evolution and stratospheric success of New Zealand's national rugby team known as the All-Blacks.

Winners of the 2011 and 2015 Rugby League World Cups, the All-Blacks epitomize how Whañau, which is a Maori (the Maori are the Polynesian people of New Zealand) word that translates as "family," can be the foundation for an elite, championship team. Whañau was not just the foundation of the Penn basketball program, but also the mantra.

I soon learned that a group chant of "Whañau" would take place after every practice, team meeting, and huddle during games. Players, coaches, and team managers would converge together in a tight circle, raise their hands high above their heads and exclaim, "Whañau!"

Let the Building Begin
First Team Meeting: July 23, 2015

"People are at their very best when they take healthy risks and they let themselves be vulnerable. The best way to understand what I'm talking about is to start talking to each other in a real way. Real communication requires having the courage to be honest and look your teammate in the eye and tell him how you feel. We will confront each other with care and respect this year. We will hold each other accountable. We will work our butts off to be the one team in the country that doesn't allow petty jealousies and resentments derail us from our goals. We will see the big picture, appreciate the opportunity to give to and serve each other, and the university. We will create a real, genuinely positive energy. We will do this starting now.

So who wants to start? What is a fear or worry that you have about this year, about yourself, or about the team?"

The six players sitting in the team room (the rest hadn't yet returned to campus) received my remarks with surprising openness. A veteran player immediately launched into his fear that he would not be fully respected as a team leader due to his history of being quiet and avoiding conflict.

His concerns were met with what can only be described as incredible support from his five teammates. Each player gave him feedback that was both supportive and validating. "We need you. We believe in you. There's no doubt you can lead us," was the essence of the feedback.

"So, what can you do differently this season," I asked. The meeting was off and running. The group listened to each other intently as each player took a turn to share their concerns about the year ahead while taking ownership of what they lacked the previous season.

Over the next couple of weeks all of the players returned to campus. The meetings became increasingly energized as they talked more and more about themselves, specifically their individual issues and goals, but also about their strengths and backgrounds.

"I've learned more about these guys in the last hour than I did all of last season," a sophomore said at the end of an August meeting. This particular session was highlighted by an intense, to say the least, discussion of different leadership styles. Players with an "in your face," confrontational style and guys with a more laid back, "lead by example" style engaged in a spirited debate.

I was able to take this opportunity to guide the communication. Empathy (getting fully into another person's shoes and honoring their point of view without defending your own); active listening; and confronting with care and respect were highlighted and processed thoroughly by session's end.

And the "I" statement was introduced. An "I" statement is a statement that begins with "I." It is a profoundly simple, extraordinarily effective way to communicate. "I" statements greatly diminish the combativeness and negative energy that is produced by "you" statements.

Let's look at an example from the team's leadership discussion:

Player A: "You just have to learn how to speak up. You gotta get in people's faces sometimes. Come on, you should know better by this point. Your style won't cut it. I do it all the time. I know how to get a guy's attention. You need to step it up."

Now, this "you statement" style is a formula for creating conflict and defensiveness. Player B, predictably, responded with the following: "That's ridiculous!" You never shut up. You don't know anything about me. You gotta learn to chill out."

The "I" statement edit:

Player A to Player B: "I want to say something that I feel strongly about but I want it to lead to somewhere productive. I know you are a lot quieter than me and we've had our differences in the past. I really want us, as a team, to let go of what went down last year. I want us all to be on the same page. I feel you have the ability to speak up, to get after guys more . . . because we need you to be more of an emotional leader. I believe in you, but you need to get better. How can we all help?"

Player B to Player A: "I know I need to step up. I appreciate what we're doing here. I'm ready. I mean, I know I can do it. I'll prove it to you and everyone here."

Every team meeting from that point through our last final postseason session in April of 2016 ended with each player sitting in our familiar circle, making an "I" statement.

"I" statements varied tremendously from meeting to meeting but the most common refrains included:

"I love everyone here."

"I believe in my brothers."

"I am so grateful to be in this family."

"I want to win this weekend."

"I'm here for you guys, all the time."

"I know we are growing something special."

"I know we work harder than any other team, it's our time now."

As Coach Donahue and his staff taught and demonstrated the core values of unity, competiveness, humility, passion, and gratitude both on and off the court, the weekly team meetings enhanced each players understanding of what it means to be in a team driven culture.

These extraordinary young student-athletes respected each other by normalizing real communication. They routinely build each other up by giving unconditional support and encouragement. Sometimes this came through confronting with care and directly holding each other accountable for poor performances. They began a new era in Penn basketball. The big picture of giving and serving, being humble and incredibly grateful, became the norm. Each individual team member understood he was part of something extraordinary: A Team Driven Culture that was just getting started.

"Whañau!"

Positive Psychology

Throughout this book, the ZONEfulness® model has presented strategies designed to connect with the peak performance zone that lives inside of each person. The Big Three of Peak Performance and the incorporation of zone exercises into a student-athletes mental strength training routine are extremely effective tools in which to access and maintain optimal play.

The final fourth technique—Gratitude and Giving Back—teaches us about the positive energy that exists all around us. A guaranteed way to harness this universal energy is to practice gratitude and to give back to the world.

Solution-Oriented Questions: Gratitude and Giving Back

I have used the following questions when teaching student-athletes about the immense power of Gratitude and Giving Back:

- "When you graduate in May, what will the underclassmen remember most about you as a leader?"

- "Have you ever given back to younger soccer players at a summer camp? If so, how did it feel to be a coach and mentor?"

- "Has your lacrosse team ever participated in community service? If so, what did you do and how did it go?"

- "What does the concept of gratitude mean to you? Do you have anyone in your life that has taught you about gratitude and giving and serving in the community?"

- "What coaches have had the most positive effect on you from Little League to the present?"

- "Have you ever imagined what it would be like to start your day focusing on the people in your life that you're most grateful for? If not, tell me what you think will happen? How would your energy shift? How about your mood? Do you think it would help you become a better softball player?"

Strategic Assignments: Gratitude and Giving Back

- "Before weight training today I want you to take two minutes and go into your gratitude zone. Specifically, close your eyes and take five really slow, deep breaths. Throughout the zone simply allow yourself to be grateful for the family members, friends, coaches, and teammates who helped you achieve your goal of earning a college football scholarship. Lift for them today!"

- "I want you to approach at least three of your teammates after practice and tell them what you feel they did well during the workout. Let them know what you appreciate about them as teammates. Demonstrate that, as captain, you see everything, not just the negative. You can create a positive energy and a winning environment by giving meaningful feedback to the team."

- "I'm really impressed with how you've approached your final season as a college lacrosse player. If you were to imagine coming back next season and were asked to address the team before a big game, what would you tell them about the importance of being grateful?"

- "I know you have described yourself as 'self-absorbed' in some of our past meetings. I also know that you don't necessarily like yourself when you get that way. So, since we will not be seeing each other for a few months I want to give you a summer long homework assignment. Here it is: Find somewhere at home to volunteer. Maybe at a basketball camp or a hospital, just do something to give to and serve others. I'll look forward to hearing from you to find out how well it's going."

Round 4: The Toxic Three versus Gratitude and Giving Back

I have talked extensively about The Toxic Three of Poor Performance: Self-Criticism, Why-ning, and What-ifing. I'm hopeful, at this point in the book, that it has been made exceedingly clear that The Big Three of Peak Performance: Extreme Self-Support, Personal History of Success, and Future Memories of Success can blow away The Toxic Three when permitted into the game.

The Final Fourth Tool: Gratitude and Giving Back is, quite simply, a performance enhancer. Whether it's your sport, academics, or the game of life, Gratitude and Giving Back is something that you can master rapidly.

"Thank you 'why' (negative focus on the past) for reminding me to be grateful for my teammates and the opportunity to play on this team."

"Thank you 'what-if' (negative focus on the future) for triggering me to be the leader I know I can be. Thank you for reminding me to give back to the younger guys and create the positive energy that this team needs."

"Thank you self-criticism for reminding me to appreciate the unbelievable support I have received from my family, coaches, and teammates to get to this point in my college career."

The combination of being grateful and giving back to others will enable you to get out of your own way (overthinking, analyzing, agonizing) while more seamlessly enabling you to access and accelerate peak performance. It is a sure-fire way to see the big picture in life and to create positive energy and emotion.

So, give back to friends and teammates by supporting them and really listening to what's going on in their lives. Use your unique skill set to help young athletes or simply volunteer at a hospital or community center. Do anything that demonstrates that you are genuinely grateful for all that you have received and achieved.

Enjoy stepping into your gratitude zone!

ZONEfulness®: A CASE STUDY
JAMAL LEWIS: "SECOND CHANCE"

In August of 2015 I had my first individual session with University of Pennsylvania senior point guard, Jamal Lewis. Greeting me with a big smile and a palpable positive energy, Jamal and I exchanged pleasantries over the course of our first five minutes together.

I had noticed that he hadn't played at all throughout his junior season and asked him what had happened.

I learned over the next 45 minutes that Jamal had suffered a life transforming traumatic illness that should have taken his life.

He explained, "My sophomore season had ended in March of 2014 and we had a little time off. I got really sick. I remember it was March 25th. I don't remember much more, but I couldn't move my arms and knew I was too weak to walk when I called the student health center. They sent a van to pick me up but the next thing I knew I was in the ER.

I remember them telling me they thought I had some type of virus but then they said that my parents really should come up to the hospital. I was thinking, 'Wow, this must be serious.' Apparently, my whole body turned bright red, then they had to put me on a respirator for six days to medically induce a coma. They found out it was a staph infection, but a very rare strain. It was called the toxic shock strain of staff infection.

Typically, people don't survive. Imagine being a parent in that situation. At one point my parents wanted everyone (in the family) to be there just in case I was about to take my last breath."

I learned that Jamal was in the Intensive Care Unit at the University of Pennsylvania hospital for ten days over the course of his 21 day stay. He spoke thoughtfully about the immense support he received from his family, friends, and his brothers from the Penn basketball team.

After a most difficult (and ongoing) road to recovery, both emotionally and physically, Jamal returned to campus for his junior year. We talked about the unfortunately common condition of survivor guilt that afflicts people who make it through life-threatening experiences when others don't survive. Jamal's good friend and aunt both lost their respective battles with cancer while Jamal was beginning his recovery.

"It was a major struggle but I learned to let go of things I can't control. I started to understand that I could control giving 100%. I wanted to maximize my effort in life. I focused on treating people the right way even when I didn't necessarily feel like it. I knew I had been given a second chance and was going to take advantage of the opportunity.

I know I took shortcuts prior to getting sick. I was more worried about results instead of giving 100%. I used to rely on physical talent, but with basketball I could have given more effort. The same thing happened in school sometimes, and with relationships.

Now, I feel appreciative. I'm grateful. I enjoy things like breathing! I'm just blessed because I wasn't supposed to survive that infection. I wasn't supposed to get back in shape to play but I've been able to do that. Before I got sick, I took for granted the personal interaction. Now I live in the moment and try to do everything I can to the best of my ability.

If I'm having lunch with someone, I'm 100% there instead of texting. You never know what may happen. Tomorrow is not a promise. You never know what will happen and when it will be taken away."

Jamal was named one of the two co-captains for the 2015-16 Penn Quakers basketball team. He demonstrated great passion and perseverance throughout the season both on and off the court. Jamal was the definition of a team driven player even though he received limited playing time.

He told me after the season, "I had the opportunity to be part of this family my senior year. I'm so incredibly grateful. I can step back and fully know that there are much more important things in life than playing time."

I am grateful for his role in our weekly team meetings. He was a true emotional leader who cared deeply about his teammates. His final "I" statement: "I am so grateful to have been with you all. I love you all. I thank you."

Jamal will pursue his higher purpose of giving and serving society as he begins the next part of his journey. In September of 2016 he will begin graduate school at Columbia University. He will work toward a master's degree in public health (M.P.H.) at the prestigious Mailmen School of Public Health in Columbia's Environmental Sciences department.

4 Techniques to Access and Master Your Zone

A FINAL ZONE EXERCISE:
THE GRATITUDE ZONE

Recently, having spent some fun, quality time with my mother, sister, and wife, I decided to have them star in my morning gratitude zone. After breathing slowly and deeply for about 30 seconds I shifted into easy, natural, rhythmic breathing. At this point I began reviewing my life experiences with the three most important women in my life, one at a time.

When I opened my eyes I was surprised that 6 minutes had gone by, having planned to do a two or three minute power zone. What I loved most was experiencing the multitude of memories, some of which I hadn't thought about since my childhood, as they seamlessly unfolded.

Playing catch with my little sister, Michelle, when she was in first grade (Michelle is 23 years younger than me); walking the beach in Cancun, Mexico with my mom; and sitting on the dock of the bay in Avalon, New Jersey with my wife, Lisa—there were just a few of the highlights of this gratitude-infused zone experience.

I really enjoy picking something or someone in my life and zoning in on how much it or they mean to me. I can best describe the feeling as liberating, freeing me to know that I am part of a much bigger picture, a universe that invites me to give . . . and then to receive . . . encouraging me to be my best self.

Try it out. I know you'll be grateful.

ACKNOWLEDGEMENTS

Joseph P. Dowling, Sr., and Eve Dowling, naturally gifted parents, thank you for your unconditional love, tireless support, and special friendship.

Sandy and Michelle Dowling, thank you both for the great past and future memories.

This book would not have been possible without the extraordinary talent and contribution of my editor-in-chief, and more importantly, great friend, Matt Conway. Thank you, Matt, for patiently navigating the project from beginning to end and directing me to the finish line.

I am indebted to the late, great Dr. Nick Rosa, an iconic professor, psychologist, peak performance pioneer, and man. Thank you, Nick, for dragging me into my best self and for your generosity on so many levels.

Dr. Janet Sasson Edgette, thank you for your brilliant supervision, your mentoring, and ongoing friendship. I was strikingly unaware of how much you were teaching me as your associate. I am so grateful.

Dr. John Edgette, thank you for allowing me to take up residence at The Milton H. Erickson Institute of Philadelphia for 20 years. Your generosity changed my life and activated my capacity to believe in myself.

Thank you, Dr. Jeff Zeig, for teaching me how to BE a therapist… Your initial greeting of "How did you get so young?" continues to resonate within me. I remain grateful for your past, present, and future friendship.

"Keep Going!" Bill O'Hanlon's mantra of encouragement reverberated within me throughout the book project. Thank you, Bill, for your course, coaching, and communication of unwavering belief.

The teachings, genius, and personhood of Milton H. Erickson, M.D., are the life blood of ZONEfulnesss. I am beyond grateful for all that I've learned and continue to learn about an Ericksonian approach.

Steve Donahue, thank you for the extraordinary opportunity to be part of the Penn family as well as for your commitment to coaching student-athletes to compete with honor and integrity in the game of life.

Kim Lewis, graphic designer and creative force extraordinaire, thank you for pulling it all together.

REFERENCES

The teachings, workshops, and writings of the following were influential in the development of *ZONEfulness: The Ultimate Guide for Student Athletes*.

Milton H. Erickson, M.D.

Jeffrey Zeig, Ph.D.

Bill O'Hanlon, M.A., LPC

Michelle Weiner-Davis, M.S.W.

Carol Hicks, M.A., L.M.F.T.

Stephen Gilligan, Ph.D.

Janet Edgette, Psy.D.

Steve de Shazer, M.S.W.

John Edgette, Psy,D.

Nicholas Rosa, Ph.D.

Lew Morgan, Ph.D.

U2
(Paul Hewson; David Evans; Adam Clayton; Larry Mullen, Jr.)

ABOUT THE AUTHOR

Joe is a licensed professional counselor who conducts his private psychology practice in Philadelphia, PA. He has worked extensively with athletes on the high school, collegiate, and professional levels for over 20 years. He is the peak performance/mental strength trainer for the University of Pennsylvania basketball program. Joe also works with the Penn baseball, softball, and women's lacrosse programs.

Joe facilitates sport psychology workshops for teams as well as peak performance seminars for corporate professionals. He sees clients out of his home office where he lives with his wife, Lisa.